Embellish
WITH RELISH

MARIA WHITEHEAD MBE
WITH FOREWORD BY NIGEL BARDEN

Hawkshead Relish: An Introduction

By Nigel Barden

Hawkshead Relish is an enterprising company led by the inspirational Whitehead family. They are a focused, driven crew and deservedly appreciated way beyond the Cumbrian borders. Their extensive range is well curated and meticulously produced, managing to capture the essence of its Lake District surroundings. It's no surprise that the founders, Maria and Mark Whitehead, have had MBEs bestowed upon them. They're inventive and fabulous ambassadors for Cumbria and its produce. As a company, Hawkshead Relish beautifully illustrates how to base your livelihood where you wish to live and reflect your surroundings. Being located in such a remarkable and rugged part of the UK, why wouldn't you make a virtue of operating out of a 16th century barn next to the beautiful expanse of Esthwaite Water.

The Hawkshead range reflects the humour which pervades the company; the ability of Mark — the Gandalf of the preserve world — to make seemingly outlandish combinations tasty and commercially viable is pure genius. His Strawberry Daiquiri Jam and Mojito Marmalade are two good examples. Having spent large chunks of my life in Cumbria as a schoolboy, a teenage tree surgeon and a twenty-something wine merchant, I'm very familiar with the vernacular. La'al is Cumbrian for small, and warmly evoked in Hawkshead's range of smaller, or la'al, jars. It's pronounced 'lie-el' and my tree surgeon mate Dennis from Staveley, near Kendal, famously used to say "Nige, we'll go into Kendal for a la'al bit and have a couple of jars"... of ale, not preserves though! Many hours or sometimes days later, full of Hartleys and Jennings bitter, we'd return to Dennis' house which he shared with his mum. The inevitable full Cumbrian brekkie that awaited us lives long in the memory. I never expected to discover another Cumbrian connection, but finding out that Mark's father, Alan, and my dad, David, grew up in Bury together has drawn me even more strongly to Hawkshead and this remarkable company.

The Westmorland Chutney, Beetroot & Horseradish Chutney and Raspberry & Vanilla Jam featured in this book are just a few other tasty examples of Mark's ingenuity and talent. On my cookery slot with Simon Mayo on Radio 2, we were bowled over by Hawkshead's Black Garlic Ketchup. Never has garlic, slow-roasted for days at a low heat, tasted so remarkable: rich, intense and the perfect partner for cheese and cold meats. Pair it with Hawkshead's Bloody Mary Ketchup and you have a duo of desert island essentials. And don't get me started on the Black Garlic Pickle! No wonder it gleaned three stars at the Great Taste Awards. In fact, Hawkshead products have picked up more than 60 Great Taste Awards to date. Mark and Maria's relationship with Halen Môn, the Anglesey sea salt company, is a union of two long established artisan families and has inevitably resulted in some magnificent offerings too (Salted Caramel Sauce to name but one).

Maria and Mark are celebrating 20 years in the business by publishing *Embellish with Relish* in tandem with talented chef Martin Frickel, and I look forward to cooking up some of the dishes with Simon Mayo on air at our new home, Scala Radio. My role in life is to champion artisan producers and Hawkshead is exactly the type of company to exalt. The founders, their daughters Abbie and Izzy, and the whole Hawkshead Relish team should be proud of their huge achievements. To capture something of the World Heritage Site that is the Lake District in every one of the 5,000 jars they turn out daily by hand is pretty remarkable.

Dedication

This book is dedicated to;

Nana (Betty Whitehead)

Grinal (Brenda Seddon)

Granby (Tom Seddon)

Acknowledgements

Mark Whitehead – husband, best friend, chief recipe tester and advisor in all things.

Izzy & **Abbie Whitehead** – long suffering daughters who tell me in no uncertain terms when I am wrong, or being embarrassing, but above all make me laugh and keep me sane!

Martin Frickel – without whom this book would not have happened: for his recipes, testing, cooking, laughter, advice and friendship.

Catherine Connor – for her artistic insight, styling and seeing the beauty in all my old pots, pans and spoons!

Richard Axford, head of the Culinary Team at Kendal College, and the students – whose willingness to allow his students to help with recipe testing and creating dishes for photography was exceptional.

Tim Green – our photographer, who remained a joy to work with throughout long days and challenging venues. He saw the vision and worked with us to get the most amazing pictures.

Phil, **Paul** and **Katie** at Meze Publishing – I can honestly say they have made a long-held wish of mine come true; I've wanted to do this for so many years and never dreamt it would happen. The Meze team have been just a pleasure to work with.

Greg Stephenson – his help behind the scenes to get the whole project off the ground and bring the team together has been invaluable, thanks to his skill in making things happen.

Karen & **David Warren** – for being there, encouraging and supporting us throughout the whole process, and eating their way through most of the recipes!

Thomas Seddon – my brother, whose knowledge of the book world has been a great help, but also his recollections of most of these family recipes which have been adapted slightly for the book.

Thanks to **Martin** and **Siobhan** of Miles Moore Ceramics for lending some of their beautiful handmade pots for use in the recipe photography.

Thank you to **Aidan** from Lovingly Artisan for providing us with their great bread.

The Relish Team – a huge thank you to everyone who has given honest opinions, tried and tested all the recipes, and supported me throughout the whole project.

Contents

Black Garlic Ketchup

Baked Cod & Tomatoes	94
Black Garlic Peppered Salmon	96
Bulgarian Black Chicken	98
Mexican Ham & Egg Brunch	100
Monday Night Supper	102
Pasta Pronto	104
Wing Dings	106

Beetroot & Horseradish Chutney

Ham & Beetroot Patties	110
My Mum's Legendary Lamb Hotpot	112
Salmon & Beetroot Bake	114
Smoked Haddock & Beetroot Quiche	116

Fig & Orange Jam

Fruity Fig & Orange Gammon Steak	120
Summer Ham Hock & Asparagus Salad	122
Fig & Orange Glazed Duck	124
Fruity Fig Baklava	126
Fig & Orange Brioche Pudding	128

Raspberry & Vanilla Jam

Afternoon Tea	132
Queen of Puddings	134
Raspberry & White Chocolate Slice	136
Raspberry Bakewell Tart	138
Raspberry Cranachan	140

Salted Caramel Sauce

Banana & Salted Caramel Showstopper Cake	144
Sticky Toffee Pudding	146
Salted Caramel Apple Parcels	148
Salted Caramel Brownie	150
Salted Caramel Popcorn Slice	152

The Story of Hawkshead Relish

The story of Hawkshead Relish starts quite a while before the company was established, and is inseparable really from our family, the places we grew up, the disaster that struck the countryside during the early 2000s, and the food that Mark and myself have always loved. We took over my parents' café in the 1990s, which was in Hawkshead, and renamed it Whigs after a medieval style of bread that Mark had resurrected from an old recipe book. The café menu was based around the whigs and featured lots of local ingredients that we wanted to showcase. It was very much about telling the story behind the food; provenance was really important to us in a way that wasn't the norm back then.

We were struggling to find any condiments that reflected that same story, and the quality that we wanted not just for the café but for ourselves and our two young daughters at home. Mark began making chutneys and preserves in the winter, when business was relatively slow at the café because of the seasonal trade in the village. The first one we ever made was the Westmorland Chutney, inspired by the spices and dried fruits that first came into Cumbria via the port towns. From there, we made things that would go with our menu like fruity jams for the scones and other chutneys for the cheese and meat platters. People loved them from the beginning, especially the Westmorland Chutney, which customers were pretty much guaranteed to buy a jar of after trying the ploughman's lunch!

We were doing fine with the café and a small range of relishes, when in 2001 – just after the February half term, when trade would usually start to pick up again – it was announced that foot and mouth had been discovered in the Borders. I can remember sitting and watching the news, thinking how awful it was for the farmers, and I didn't have a clue as to how much impact the disease would have on our business. At the end of the broadcast, they said that people were advised to avoid the countryside, and I thought that seemed quite drastic, as surely only farmland would be dangerous. The next day Mark went to work, opened up, made the bread, and, a bit naively I suppose, we just assumed things would carry on as normal. We didn't have any customers at all that day, and for about another week there was nothing... it was like a Wild West film with the tumbleweed rolling through ghost towns.

Because we had borrowed money from the bank to buy the café, we had those repayments to meet, but as the trade was so seasonal then our income stream had just been completely cut off. The bank manager arranged to visit us and I thought we were going to lose everything – our home, which was above the café, and our livelihood – but he asked if we had a business plan. I told him about the relishes, we gave him some jars of it and he saw the potential we knew it had but couldn't invest in. He gave us a repayment holiday "for as long as you need to get this off the ground" and after 18 months of scraping the barrel to buy ingredients, selling at farmers' markets, and customers starting to trickle back in at the café, The Hawkshead Relish Company was properly established.

Mark in the café kitchen circa 2000.

The Relish shop in midwinter

Production facility; 16th century barn on the edge of Esthwaite

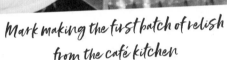

Mark making the first batch of relish
from the café kitchen

Development of the redundant farm building
into the production facility.

Mark and Maria on 'Ready Steady Cook' with Ainsley Harriot, Nick Nairn & James Tanner

Mark and Maria receiving the
Great Taste Producer of the Year Award in 2005
from Jean Christophe Novelli

It was incredibly hard work running the café as well as making enough relishes to sell. In 2002 we entered our first Great Taste Awards and didn't expect to get very far, but we won with three of our products which was very exciting. By 2005 we had won Speciality Producer of the Year and all of a sudden the company was catapulted into national visibility; we ended up going on radio programmes and even Ready Steady Cook. It was a real catalyst for change because it enabled us to supply bigger places. We initially got a few lines into Tesco, but decided it wasn't the route we wanted to go down, so we pulled out and focused on local and independent stores instead.

At that point, Mark was still making all the bread and running the café, and the girls would don aprons after school to help us with labelling. Something had to give, and so we made the huge decision to close our café and reopen the space as a relish shop. It was a gamble we didn't know would pay off until the end of the first day, when we cashed up and found we'd taken more money in that afternoon than we'd ever taken in a day at the café. That shift allowed the company to grow, but working in such a tiny production space was getting tricky, so we started to look for other premises and found a 16th century barn a mile outside of Hawkshead. It had been reroofed but was empty – beautiful, but redundant – and the owners were looking for someone who could put it to good use. There was a brewery using two small areas, but the bigger part was just stood there, waiting for us, really.

We got some grant funding and worked out what we needed to convert the barn. It was a Grade I listed building so there were a lot of hoops we had to jump through, but after six months' work we moved in and fairly quickly filled the whole space, which I'd thought we never would because it was huge. We had created a development kitchen, offices and storage which seemed like an enormous step up from our 150 litre pan in the back room of the shop, which we had only been able to get in by taking the window out! We've now got four 300 litre pans, and a few years ago we ran out of office space so we moved all our storage facilities to a unit in Ambleside, then in 2017 we took on another warehouse which is where all the labelling is done now.

We've increased our product range accordingly over the years, and have around 120 different chutneys, pickles, preserves, ketchups, jams and sauces in our repertoire. We like to dabble in everything, which is why we named the company Hawkshead Relish to begin with, so it wasn't too specific and we could be inventive in our development. We do keep paring them off, but people ask for certain products and they trickle back in again...it's all been based on demand. We've gone from making 12 jars at a time to making roughly 6000 jars a day. We will always make everything exactly as anyone would at home though, and all our recipes are devised by Mark. We don't cut corners or use cheap ingredients, there are no additives, colourings, flavourings or preservatives in anything, and our first and main baseline is 'would we put this on our table at home?'

Mark and Maria receive their MBEs at Buckingham Palace with daughters Izzy and Abbie, in November 2011

Exports have been another key part of our business growth, and we have since helped other small businesses get on their own journey to export globally. It was our work with other businesses in Cumbria and helping with DiT (Department of International Trade) that led us to both be awarded MBEs by Her Majesty The Queen in the 2011 Birthday Honours list. This was such a huge surprise to us both, and even now we feel extremely honoured and unworthy of it but equally very thrilled. We were even more excited that it was the Queen herself who presented us with our medals. We'd met her once before and she graciously said how lovely it was to see us again, which was incredibly touching. We had a fabulous day at Buckingham Palace with our daughters Abbie and Izzy and Mark's mother Betty. Sadly neither of my parents could join us, but they were all so very proud.

For Mark and I, because of what we went through to get to this point, the business is not about working our socks off to get into mass production. It's about quality of life, to be able to say everybody is really happy. The business has become much more efficient as it's evolved over the years, so we have a very tight-knit team of 25 people. This means we can reward them, make sure everyone is working to their potential, and keep growing together.

Because Hawkshead Relish is family-run, this attitude is especially important for us. Our eldest, Abbie, asked to work full time with the business over one summer, and never left! She works in the shop, helps with a lot of the buying, and enjoys the front-facing side of things. Then Izzy joined when we were short in the office during an Easter holiday. Four years on, she manages all our social media and designs our advertising, goes to trade shows, and has a complete understanding of and genuine passion for our products.

Mark is exceptional at blending flavour combinations. He has this innate ability to look at a fruit or vegetable and know instantly and instinctively which spices will work with it. He's always advocated a system which the French call terroir, which is the 'what grows together goes together' principle. When we're developing any new product, the first step is to think about where it's come from and how we're going to make it a little bit different from the rest. A good example is our Strawberry & Black Pepper Jam. When we ran the Queen's Head in Hawkshead, a group of Italian deerstalkers used to stay every year, and at the end of each meal they'd always ask for a bowl of strawberries. They'd put a little red wine in the bowl with the strawberries and grind some black pepper over the top, which I thought was very strange until I tried it, and it was mind blowing! I've never ever forgotten it, and that was why Strawberry & Black Pepper Jam came into being.

Everybody brings very different but equally valuable skills to the business, and thrives in their individual roles. I try and keep out of the kitchen and Mark tries to keep out of the office! We don't encroach on each other's space but there's always crossover, so we know that between us we've got everything covered and everyone's happy, which is our main priority both as a business and as a family for the future of Hawkshead Relish.

Mark and Maria meet
Her Majesty the Queen in 2005

HRH Prince Charles talks to sales manager
Jonathan Robb on his visit in April 2019

Travels & Inspiration

The ideas behind our products more often than not come from places we've travelled to, or even just moments on holidays when you have that extra bit of headspace that allows the creative juices to flow. Both Mark and I grew up in families that travelled abroad regularly, so we caught the bug at an early age and have explored many countries and cuisines as adults and with our own children. It's always been about the food, and learning as much as we can from everywhere we visit, whether that's Mexico, France, Vietnam, Spain, Morocco, Italy, Laos, Myanmar, Cambodia, Malaysia or Japan.

Before we started Hawkshead Relish, Mark and I travelled around India for about six weeks and it was a revelation to us. The freshness and flavour of the spices, and the ways they were used in food, had us completely enthralled. We visited a spice plantation and discovered the chutneys people were making, which were always fresh and designed to be eaten that day rather than jarred and kept for a long time. The vibrancy of those chutneys and the spices that made them were at the forefront of our minds when we came home and began making our relishes. From the beginning, we roasted and ground whole spices ourselves to extract all the flavour; you have to release the oils in order to bring them to life.

We've been back to India many times since then, and products such as our Kashmiri Tomato Chutney, Hot Garlic Pickle and Mango Chutney (which is quite traditional and a world away from the sweet gloop you might be more familiar with) are testament to how much the flavours of that country have inspired us. Mark will go into restaurant kitchens and talk to chefs about their recipes, finding out what they're using – which might be things we've never heard of – and gaining a really good understanding of flavour. One of the best experiences we had with food was in Cambodia, where we got talking to our guide and ended up cooking a meal over an open fire for his neighbours at their farm with ingredients we'd bought at the local market. The flavours of south east Asia have blown me away on our travels across the continent – it seems to be spices that we're usually drawn towards – but every time we go away new recipes or ideas will inevitably join our repertoire.

Our Family

I moved to Hawkshead from Southport, which were once both in Lancashire, when I was 15, so I think of that as my home county through and through! I'll always be an 'offcomer' but I love Hawkshead and feel very at home here. Both my parents had links to food, interestingly, as my great grandfather was Spanish and made his living exporting oranges from the Canaries to Liverpool, which is where he met my great grandmother. I'm very proud of that connection, and there's a nice synergy in the fact that I'm now making orange marmalade which is sold in Spain! My father's family are from Martin Mere which is a huge growing area, and some are still in agriculture there today. Recipes from their childhoods have resonated through mine; the new potato pie in this book is my version of one my dad used to go on and on about which his mum made originally, and my mum's lamb hotpot was a permanent fixture as I grew up.

Mark's family are foodie people too, and his mother especially had a love of travelling that was instilled in him and introduced Mark to different flavours, cultures and places. He went to catering college, following in the footsteps of his parents who had moved from Bury to the Lakes and ran pubs and restaurants, eventually taking on the Dicksons Arms in Haverthwaite which my family used to visit on a Sunday. Mark became friends with my brother, Thomas, and I would sometimes go out with them as well. One week Mark asked if I wanted to go out and I said yes, assuming he meant me and my brother as he normally did. The evening came and I saw my brother wasn't getting ready, and he said: "I'm not going – he's asked you out!" I'd had no idea, but then the doorbell went and the rest, as they say, is history.

My parents ended up buying the Dicksons Arms from his parents, so I helped run it until Mark and I got married in 1984, when I joined his family in running the Queen's Head in Hawkshead. We've always been in and around the village since then; it's a very close-knit community which really grounds you to a place. A lot of the people working for us now were at primary school together, and of course our two daughters have grown up here and are now an integral part of the business, which wouldn't be what it is without the family history and love of food that we all share.

After Mark's father died, we took his mum, Betty, to India for a trip of a lifetime. She absolutely loved it and embraced the experience even at 83 years old. Betty sadly died in 2015 still talking of her travels, her favourite foods and love of life. We talk of her often and laugh at the wonderful memories.

As I write this book, I have just lost my lovely father to Alzheimer's. My mum passed away in 2016 following a series of strokes and only then did we realise just how Dad was suffering and how much Mum had been covering things up.

They have all been very much in my heart and mind when working on this book: their joint love of food and holidays – many of which we all took together – and some fabulous memories of feasting in the Spanish sunshine. So many of these recipes are ones we have grown up with, and shared with them while laughing, talking and making these precious memories.

How To Use This Book

The idea behind this collection of recipes is to make people think a little differently about that stash of relishes most of us have sitting in the cupboard. They are – or the good ones can be – goldmines of flavour, waiting to perfectly complement your next meal or bring new depths of flavour to your favourite plateful.

Nobody wants jars of chutneys, pickles, preserves and sauces cluttering up the pantry or the fridge door, going out of date and being thrown out because they've grown a layer of mould. So let's release them! It's easier than you think to use each one in new ways that don't reinvent the wheel but work alongside your established favourites and simple but exciting dishes that draw on flavours from all over the world.

We've split the recipes into ten chapters, each starring one of our most popular Hawkshead Relish products and a few others besides. From the familiar, like Red Onion Marmalade, to one of our newest creations, the Black Garlic Ketchup, we hope everyone finds something to have a go at and enjoys recreating our versions of dishes that regularly grace our family table.

Westmorland Chutney

Westmorland Chutney was our first ever creation. We were looking for a chutney that would complement the dishes we served in our café, like Welsh Rarebit and platters of local meats and cheeses, but all the commercial condiments on offer at the time were quite harsh and vinegary.

Mark began looking through his old Lakeland cookbooks and historic documents linked to Hawkshead, one of the smallest towns in Britain, granted a market charter by King James I in 1608. Evidence of the marketplace can still be found in the old village centre, though the arches of the lower Market Hall where there was once a row of butchers shops are now filled in.

William the Conqueror's grandson, King Stephen 1st, included Hawkshead and its environs in his 1137 endowment of Furness Abbey. The monks were great entrepreneurs who ran extensive flocks of sheep on the fells; these 'sheep walks' were known by the Old Norse term 'herd-vik' (now the name of the local breed, Herdwick). For 400 years the monks developed and ran Hawkshead as a market centre for raw wool, yarn and the coarse homespun undyed cloth known as 'hodden grey' and worn by the labouring poor throughout much of northern Europe.

The diets of the residents of Hawkshead, Cumberland and Westmorland began to change quite rapidly with the development of the port of Whitehaven on the west coast, from 1630 onwards. Coal was the chief export and tobacco the chief import, along with a range of unusual herbs, spices, dried fruits, sugar and rum from Barbados with coffee and cocoa from St Lucia. These ingredients led to the creation of many dishes that remain popular today, including Cumberland Rum Nicky, a tart made with dates, brown sugar and rum, Westmorland Apple Tansy, an omelette-like pudding made with apples, nutmeg and allspice, and Westmorland Pepper Cake, made with black treacle, raisins, currants, ginger, cloves and black pepper.

Drawing on this rich heritage, Mark set about using spices and fruits to create a chutney that incorporated some of these elements. Brown sugar, prunes, dates, onions and spices such as allspice and ginger give this chutney a rich, dark and fruity finish that was perfect for serving alongside our café dishes.

Ever since then, Westmorland Chutney has always been on our bestseller list, and with good reason!

EMBELLISH
WITH RELISH
Westmorland
farmhouse chutney
HAWKSHEAD Relish COMPANY

Lancashire New Potato Pie

Preparation time: 25 minutes | Cooking time: 40 minutes | Serves: 4

My lovely dad grew up helping on his uncle's farm at Martin Mere near Southport, then in Lancashire. He often talked about the New Potato Pie so this is in homage to him and the best new potatoes you can find.

450g small new potatoes

60g butter

2 medium sliced onions

Salt and pepper

500g pack of ready-made shortcrust pastry

1 jar of Hawkshead Relish Westmorland Chutney

200g crumbled Lancashire cheese

1 egg yolk

Preheat the oven to 180°c.

Wash and then boil the new potatoes for 5 minutes in salted water then set aside to cool.

In a saucepan, melt the butter then add the onions and cook on a gentle heat until the onions are soft but not brown. Season with a little salt and lots of black pepper.

Grease and line a baking tray then roll the pastry out to a 35cm round.

Spread a good layer of Westmorland Chutney over the pastry base, leaving a 5cm gap around the edge. Once cooled, Crush the new potatoes in the palm of your hand and place them in the centre of the pie base with the onions and most of the cheese. Sprinkle the remaining cheese on top, then fold over the pastry to encase the pie and add a twist of black pepper over the top.

Brush the pastry with egg yolk and bake in the oven for around 30 minutes until the potatoes are soft and the cheese has melted.

You can adapt this recipe by adding crispy bacon pieces, softened leeks or black pudding. If you're making this out of season use small potatoes such as Charlottes instead of new potatoes.

Fruity Roast Belly Pork

Preparation time: 30 minutes | Cooking time: 3 hours | Serves: 4

Belly of pork is a sweet and succulent cut, and with a fruity sticky stuffing it's perfect for a Sunday roast. Tender meat and proper crispy crackling make this recipe a real crowd pleaser.

1.2kg pork belly (ready to roll)

Salt and pepper

2 tablespoons Hawkshead Relish Westmorland Chutney

1 diced small onion

1 chopped clove of garlic

1 tablespoon oil

180g sausage meat

5-6 fresh sage leaves

6-8 chopped ready to eat prunes

40g breadcrumbs

120g peeled and finely chopped apple

Score the skin of the pork lengthways at 1cm intervals, being careful to not go through the meat. Turn the belly skin side down on your worktop then season the meat with salt and pepper. Spread half of the Westmorland Chutney evenly across the pork, leaving a gap around the edge.

Fry the onion and garlic gently in oil until soft and then allow to cool. Mix the sausage meat, onion, garlic, sage, prunes, the remaining Westmorland Chutney and breadcrumbs in a bowl, then add the apple. Roll the stuffing into a sausage shape, place it along the centre of the pork belly, roll the pork around the stuffing and tie the joint tightly. Rub the skin with oil and lots of salt and then leave to air dry for a couple of hours. Preheat the oven to 220°c.

Place the pork on an oven tray and put into the preheated oven for 30 minutes. Drop the temperature to 170°c and continue to cook the pork for 2 hours. After this time, increase the temperature to 220°c to crisp up the crackling and then let the pork rest for 30 minutes out of the oven before carving and serving.

Serve with Hassleback potatoes; Take a whole medium potato and slice many times almost all the way through, rub over a little olive oil and sprinkle with sea salt then bake in the oven as you would a jacket potato.

Westmorland Sausage Roll

Preparation time: 10-15 minutes | Cooking time: 25-30 minutes | Serves: 4

These are ideally made with Cumberland sausages, but you can use any good sausage meat and just season it really well. You need a good amount of black pepper to complement the sweetness of the fruit that comes through from the chutney. Perfect for picnics and parties.

Olive oil

1 finely sliced red onion

A few finely chopped leaves of fresh sage

Salt and pepper

6 small Cumberland sausages

50g fresh breadcrumbs

250g puff pastry

1 jar of Hawkshead Relish Westmorland Chutney

1 beaten egg

Heat the oven to 180°c.

In a saucepan, heat the oil and gently cook the onion until soft. Add the chopped sage, season with salt and pepper and then leave to cool slightly.

Cut open the sausages and place the meat in a large mixing bowl. Add the herby onions and the breadcrumbs then mix well. It works best to use your hands here.

Roll out the pastry on a floured surface, creating a large rectangle about 1cm thick. Spread a layer of Westmorland Chutney evenly over the pastry, leaving a gap around all the edges, then shape the meat into a long sausage shape and lay this down over the Westmorland Chutney in the centre of the pastry.

Brush the beaten egg along the pastry edges then fold over and seal along one side, using a fork to press the edges together tightly. Use the egg wash for the rest of the sausage roll and then bake it in the oven for 25 to 30 minutes until the pastry is golden brown and puffed up.

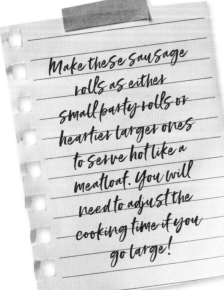

Make these sausage rolls as either small party rolls or heartier larger ones to serve hot like a meatloaf. You will need to adjust the cooking time if you go large!

Westmorland Soufflé Rarebit

Preparation time: 15 minutes | Cooking time: 10 minutes | Serves: 4

This recipe is based on a traditional Welsh Rarebit recipe that we used to serve in our café in Hawkshead back in the day. It was always a favourite and using a great sourdough bread makes all the difference.

10g butter

10g plain flour

6 tablespoons milk

½ teaspoon English mustard

2 teaspoons Hawkshead Relish Worcester Sauce

Pinch of cayenne pepper

Salt and pepper

2 eggs

55g mature cheddar cheese

1 jar of Hawkshead Relish Westmorland Chutney

6 slices of lightly toasted sourdough bread

Preheat the grill to a medium temperature while you gently melt the butter in a saucepan. Add the flour, mix until all the butter is absorbed, then gradually add the milk while stirring continuously until you have a smooth sauce.

Remove from the heat and add the mustard, Hawkshead Relish Worcester Sauce and a small sprinkle of cayenne pepper. Season to taste with salt and pepper.

Separate the eggs and beat the yolks. Slowly add these to the sauce, then add the cheese and stir until it has all melted.

Whisk the egg whites to stiff peaks then use a metal spoon to gently fold them into the cheese mixture.

Spread a good layer of Westmorland Chutney over one side of the toast and top with the cheese mixture, creating peaks to give the surface some texture.

Pop under a medium temperature grill and toast until golden brown.

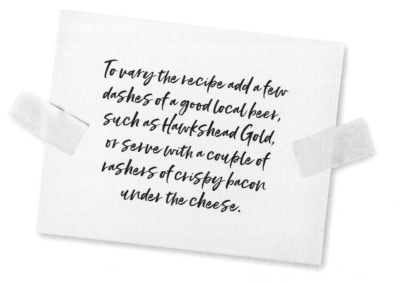

To vary the recipe add a few dashes of a good local beer, such as Hawkshead Gold, or serve with a couple of rashers of crispy bacon under the cheese.

Sticky Ribs

Preparation time: 10 minutes | Cooking time: 1 hour 40 minutes | Serves: 4

These ribs are lip-smackingly tasty: too good to keep for BBQ season as they work at any time of the year! Messy, delicious and always a crowd pleaser.

2kg meaty pork belly ribs

Salt and pepper

2 teaspoons English mustard powder

2 teaspoons paprika

2 tablespoons Hawkshead Relish Westmorland Chutney

2 tablespoons Hawkshead Relish Damson Ketchup (or Black Garlic Ketchup)

1 tablespoon Hawkshead Relish Worcester Sauce

30g dark brown sugar

400ml chicken stock

Heat the oven to 180°c. Season the ribs with salt and pepper, mustard and paprika. Mix all the remaining ingredients together in an ovenproof dish, coat the ribs and cover with a lid or tin foil.

Place the dish in the preheated oven to cook for 20 minutes, then reduce the heat to 140°c and cook for a further hour. Remove the lid and continue to cook for a further 20 minutes to crisp them up. Brush each rib with the sauce before serving to get them nice and sticky.

Always get your ribs from the butchers if you can; this way you will get some meaty ribs that really give flavour.

Red Onion Marmalade

Traditionally, marmalade is made with citrus fruits, and the name derives from the Portuguese word marmelada, which refers to the quince (marmelo) jam they make.

However, food is always developing and evolving and over the last 30 years or so, onion marmalade has become a household staple.

It's thought to have originated in France with a confit d'oignon, which basically means cooking the onion until it caramelises in its own sugars, which are released through a long slow cooking process.

Hawkshead Relish were one of the first UK producers to bring out a Red Onion Marmalade. Ours is made with balsamic vinegar, redcurrants and raisins. It is sweet with complex layers of flavour from the herbs and spices we use, along with the fruity caramelisation from our long slow cooking process.

EMBELLISH
WITH RELISH

Red
Onion
marmalade

HAWKSHEAD *Relish* COMPANY

Betty's Braised Beef & Onions

Preparation time: 20 minutes | Cooking time: 2 hours | Serves: 4

Whenever Mark's mother Betty came to visit she would put this in the oven, and when we got in from work the aroma would have us salivating. It's proper comfort food! I have adapted it slightly but I know she would approve, as long as there is plenty of black pepper.

3 tablespoons sunflower oil

4 sliced medium onions

4 braising steaks (about 200g each)

500ml beef stock (made with 1 stock cube if using)

1 crushed clove of garlic

2 tablespoons Hawkshead Relish Red Onion Marmalade

1 tablespoon Hawkshead Relish Black Garlic Ketchup

½ teaspoon English mustard powder

1 tablespoon chopped fresh thyme

1 bay leaf

Salt and pepper

Preheat the oven to 170°c.

Heat the oil in a large frying pan, add the onions and cook until soft but not browned. Remove the onions from the pan, add the pieces of steak, brown them on all sides and then set aside.

Mix the beef stock with the garlic, Red Onion Marmalade, Black Garlic Ketchup and mustard powder, then add the herbs and season with salt and pepper.

Place the onions and meat in a large casserole dish and pour over the stock. Cover tightly with a lid or tin foil and bake in the oven for at least 1 hour 30 minutes, or 2 hours, until the meat is very tender and you can't bear to wait any longer!

Serve with seasonal vegetables and garlic mashed potato.

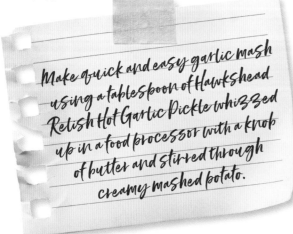

Make quick and easy garlic mash using a tablespoon of Hawkshead Relish Hot Garlic Pickle whizzed up in a food processor with a knob of butter and stirred through creamy mashed potato.

Aubergine & Red Onion Bake

Preparation time: 30 minutes | Cooking time: 45 minutes | Serves: 4

Baking instead of frying the aubergine will reduce the amount of fat needed in this dish. It's very versatile and you can stuff the rolls with your own Bolognese sauce instead of the ricotta and spinach.

2 aubergines

2 tablespoons olive oil

Knob of butter

1 finely chopped onion

1 finely chopped clove of garlic

500g baby spinach

250g tub of ricotta

2 tablespoons Hawkshead Relish Red Onion Marmalade

Salt and pepper

2 tins of chopped tomatoes

1 teaspoon mixed dried herbs

4 tablespoons fresh white breadcrumbs

200g grated mozzarella

Heat the oven to 220°c and slice the aubergines lengthways into roughly half centimetre thickness.

Brush both sides of the aubergine with oil and bake in the oven for 12 to 15 minutes until tender, turning over halfway through.

In a small pan, melt the butter with a little olive oil, add the onion and cook until soft but not coloured, then add the garlic and cook gently for another minute. Add the spinach leaves, remove from the heat and set aside to cool. Drain off any watery liquid and transfer to a large bowl. Mix in the ricotta and Red Onion Marmalade then season with a little salt and pepper.

Place a teaspoon of the filling onto each of the aubergine slices and roll them up, then put them into an ovenproof dish with the join facing down. Pour over the chopped tomatoes, sprinkle over the dried herbs and drizzle with olive oil. Mix together the breadcrumbs and grated mozzarella and sprinkle over the top.

Bake in the oven for 25 to 30 minutes until golden brown and piping hot.

Serve with a fresh green salad.

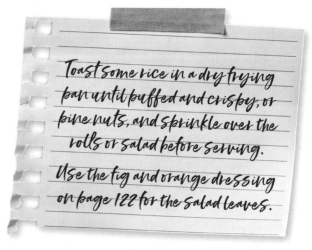

Toast some rice in a dry frying pan until puffed and crispy, or pine nuts, and sprinkle over the rolls or salad before serving.

Use the fig and orange dressing on page 122 for the salad leaves.

Mackerel with Caramelised Onion

Preparation time: 20 minutes | Cooking time: 12 minutes | Serves: 4

We both love fish, and this dish would work well with any oily fish. We've had it with salmon, tuna and sea bass. The dish would also be lovely on a bed of Puy lentils or with cauliflower purée.

2 tablespoons olive oil

4 tablespoons Hawkshead Relish Red Onion Marmalade

1 tablespoon raisins, soaked in 2 tablespoons (30ml) white wine vinegar

8 mackerel fillets (pin-boned if possible)

Salt and pepper

1 small sliced onion

1 tablespoon pine nuts

Chopped fresh parsley

1 lemon

Heat the oven to 190°c.

Combine the olive oil, Red Onion Marmalade and soaked raisins, along with the vinegar soaking liquor and a little water.

Put the mixture in an ovenproof dish and place the fish skin side up on top, then season with salt and pepper and brush a little oil onto the skin. Place in the oven for 8 minutes until the fish is just cooked. To crisp the fish skin, place under a hot grill for a further 4 minutes until golden.

Meanwhile, fry the sliced onion in oil until crispy and toast the pine nuts in a dry pan until browned.

Serve the fish with the sauce spooned over the top, and finish with a few sprinkles of crispy onions, toasted pine nuts and chopped parsley. Place a wedge of lemon on each plate.

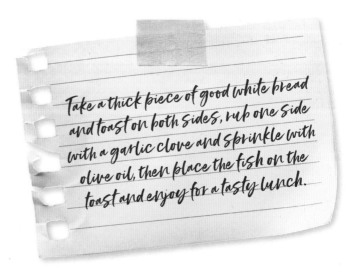

Take a thick piece of good white bread and toast on both sides, rub one side with a garlic clove and sprinkle with olive oil, then place the fish on the toast and enjoy for a tasty lunch.

Sausage & Bean Hotpot

Preparation time: 10 minutes | Cooking time: 45 minutes | Serves: 4

A hearty supper dish filled with tomatoes, beans and vegetables. I have made this with chicken thighs as well and it's a great alternative. Serve with a hunk of sourdough bread.

4 chopped sticks of celery

4 chopped carrots

2 chopped onions

6 chopped cloves of garlic

2 sprigs of rosemary

4 tablespoons light olive oil

2 tins of chopped tomatoes

1 tablespoon of tomato purée

300ml chicken stock

4 tablespoons Hawkshead Relish Red Onion Marmalade

2 tablespoons Hawkshead Relish Honey Mustard

1 tablespoon Hawkshead Relish Worcester Sauce

Salt and pepper

800g drained and rinsed cannellini beans

12 small Cumberland sausages

Preheat the oven to 180°c.

Cook the celery, carrots, onion, garlic and rosemary in olive oil for about 5 to 10 minutes on a medium heat. Add the tomatoes, tomato purée, chicken stock, Red Onion Marmalade, Honey Mustard, Worcester Sauce, salt and pepper then cook for 5 minutes. Add the beans, give everything a good stir, then transfer the mixture to an ovenproof dish.

In a frying pan add a teaspoon of oil and brown the sausages then place them on top of the hotpot and bake for 20 minutes in the preheated oven. When the 20 minutes are up, give the hotpot a stir and return to the oven for a further 10 minutes.

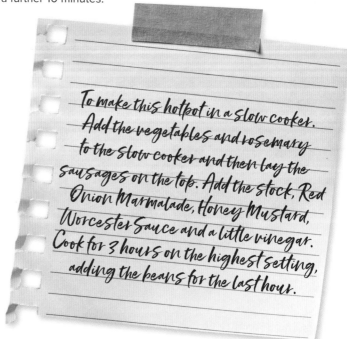

To make this hotpot in a slow cooker. Add the vegetables and rosemary to the slow cooker and then lay the sausages on the top. Add the stock, Red Onion Marmalade, Honey Mustard, Worcester Sauce and a little vinegar. Cook for 3 hours on the highest setting, adding the beans for the last hour.

Greek Minted Lamb Burgers

Preparation time: 20-25 minutes | Cooking time: 20-30 minutes | Serves: 4

I love Lakeland lamb, so much so it was served at our wedding in 1984! These burgers are very juicy and the mint really comes through. With the salty feta cheese and salad leaves it's a great dish; you could make the burgers into meatballs and serve with couscous and salad on the side.

For the burger

500g lean lamb mince

10g chopped mint

10g chopped parsley

3 tablespoons Hawkshead Relish Red Onion Marmalade

1 tablespoon lemon juice

Salt and pepper

2 tablespoons olive oil

4 burger buns

50g spinach

1 pack of crumbled feta

1 sliced small red onion

2 teaspoons sherry vinegar

10-12 mint leaves for the salad

For the chips

1kg Maris Piper potatoes

Vegetable oil, for frying

Halen Môn sea salt and vinegar seasoning

Generous pinch of chopped rosemary

For the burger

Mix the lamb mince, mint, parsley, Red Onion Marmalade, lemon juice, and a good pinch of salt and pepper together. Shape into four 7 to 10cm thick patties.

Put one and a half tablespoons of the oil in a non-stick pan and cook the patties over a medium heat for about 2 to 4 minutes on each side. You can finish them off in the oven if they brown too quickly.

Meanwhile, preheat the grill and toast the buns until golden for about 2 minutes. Place a burger on the bottom half of each bun. Toss the spinach, feta, onion, vinegar, mint leaves and the remaining oil in a bowl. Place the salad on top of the burgers and top with a tablespoon of Red Onion Marmalade. Press firmly to compact them.

For the chips

Cut the potatoes with skins still on into thick chips, then par-boil them for 5 to 8 minutes dependant on the size of the chips. Drain and leave to air dry, then fry in hot oil for around 4 minutes until golden brown and crispy. Sprinkle the chips with the Halen Môn seasoning and chopped rosemary.

Try rolling the meat mixture around a skewer instead of making a burger, or make tiny meatballs and serve with rice. You could also make a dressing using Greek yoghurt flavoured with chopped mint and cucumber pieces.

Cheese & Onion Flatbreads

Preparation time: 1 hour 35 minutes | Cooking time: 10-15 minutes | Serves: 4

These are surprisingly quick and easy to make, I like to use Wensleydale cheese but you can adapt to use what you have available, great for dipping into hummus and with a lovely bowl of French Onion Soup.

500g strong white bread flour

10g salt

10g instant yeast

30g softened unsalted butter

310ml warm water

2 tablespoons Hawkshead Relish Red Onion Marmalade

250g crumbled Wensleydale cheese

Splash of olive oil

Knob of melted butter

Fresh chopped parsley

Put the flour in a large bowl with the salt on one side and the yeast on the other, so that the salt doesn't kill the yeast. Add the butter and three quarters of the water. Bring the ingredients together with your fingers, adding a little more water if required.

Tip the dough onto a lightly floured surface and knead. Keep kneading for 5 to 10 minutes, working until it becomes soft. This can also be done with a mixer and dough hook. When the dough is ready, transfer it to a lightly oiled bowl and leave it to double in size. This should take between 1 hour and 1 hour 30 minutes.

Tip the proved dough onto a floured surface and fold several times to knock the air out. Divide into eight pieces. Roll each piece out with a floured rolling pin, making them roughly the same shape and size. Spread four of the rounds with Red Onion Marmalade and cover with a sprinkle of cheese, then place a second round over the top and press the two together.

Heat a frying pan with a little olive oil over a medium to high heat. Fry each flatbread for 2 to 3 minutes on each side until golden brown and puffy.

Brush the cooked flatbreads with melted butter and scatter with parsley. Serve warm.

Swap the parsley for chopped coriander and serve with a curry

Hot Garlic Pickle

Over the years, Mark and I have travelled to India with our daughters in search of spices, recipes and of course a little mid-winter warmth.

This pickle was developed after a trip to Madras, during which we ate at a restaurant that served up a main course heavily seasoned with garlic and spices. The flavours were astounding, and Mark's notebook immediately came out; he was convinced that it would work as a pickle.

As soon as we got back to the UK Mark started work on it, recreating those amazing flavours by gently cooking garlic cloves to the point where they are soft but still whole and flavoursome...simply delicious! The resulting pickle contains chilli, mustard seeds, turmeric and cayenne pepper, but doesn't contain fenugreek, which would give it a typical 'curry' flavour.

It's a really versatile condiment that you can serve alongside a range of dishes, or you can simply cook with it to create real depth of flavour. Just by adding a few key ingredients, you can create dishes from a range of cuisines from around the world, including North Africa and the Far East.

At home we blend Hot Garlic Pickle into creamed potatoes for a quick garlic mash, combine it with butter and spread over flatbreads to create a spicy garlic bread, or make a simple garlic mayonnaise by crushing the pickle into mayonnaise and stirring well.

We always have at least one jar of this on the go at home; it's a perfect cupboard staple.

EMBELLISH
WITH RELISH

taste

Hot
Garlic
pickle

HAWKSHEAD *Relish* COMPANY

Chicken & Apricot Curry

Preparation time: 15 minutes | Cooking time: 40 minutes | Serves: 4

Having spent such a long time in India over the years, the British curry is a very different beast to anything you would come across over there, so this is an adaptation of a real authentic Indian classic dish that we have enjoyed in northern India on many occasions. It's so easy to make and really tasty, you could adapt it by swapping the chicken for prawns or cubed Indian paneer cheese.

1 teaspoon whole cardamom pods

1 teaspoon coriander seeds

1 teaspoon cumin seeds

2 tablespoons Hawkshead Relish Hot Garlic Pickle

1 teaspoon vegetable oil

6 skinned and boned chicken thighs

1 sliced large onion

1 tin of chopped tomatoes

1 finely chopped red chilli

1 tablespoon white wine or rice vinegar

8-10 quartered dried apricots

To serve

Fresh coriander

Crispy onions

Nigella seeds

Warm flatbreads

Lightly crush the cardamom pods then toast them with the coriander and cumin seeds in a dry frying pan on a medium heat, until they start to colour and release oils and flavour.

Blend the Hot Garlic Pickle to a paste in a food processor, or using a mortar and pestle. Add the warmed spices and combine.

Put the vegetable oil in the frying pan and add the spiced garlic paste. Cook until hot but don't let it burn, then add the chicken and stir to coat the meat. Add the onion followed by the tomatoes, chilli and a splash of vinegar.

Reduce the heat and allow to simmer for 20 to 30 minutes until the chicken is cooked through. Add the dried apricots and, if necessary, a little water or chicken stock then cook for a further 5 minutes.

Check the seasoning; you can add more chilli at this point according to your preference.

Serve with freshly chopped coriander, crispy onions, nigella seeds and warm flatbreads.

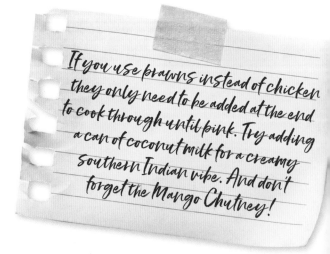

If you use prawns instead of chicken they only need to be added at the end to cook through until pink. Try adding a can of coconut milk for a creamy southern Indian vibe. And don't forget the Mango Chutney!

Spiced Garlic Kiev

Preparation time: 15-20 minutes | Cooking time: 20 minutes | Serves: 4

Once you master the art of cutting a pinhole into a chicken breast and stuffing it, you can experiment with lots of different ideas. I love this one with the garlic and spices; it's fragrant but the garlic doesn't linger too long afterwards.

4 skinned chicken breasts

2 tablespoons crushed Hawkshead Relish Hot Garlic Pickle

125g softened butter

Chopped fresh parsley

For the coating

2 large beaten eggs

100g plain flour

Salt and pepper

140g fresh white breadcrumbs

4 tablespoons sunflower oil

Heat the oven to 200°c.

With a sharp knife, make an incision in the top edge of the thickest part of the chicken breast, then use the knife to open a pouch inside the flesh without making the entry hole any larger. Repeat for all the chicken breasts.

Blend the crushed Hot Garlic Pickle with 100g of the butter then mix in the chopped parsley and transfer the flavoured butter into a small piping bag (you can make one from a small plastic food bag with one of the corners snipped off). Pipe the mixture into the hole in the chicken breast and seal with a cocktail stick. Repeat for all the chicken breasts.

For the coating

Place the beaten egg in a large bowl, put the flour on a large flat plate and season it with salt and pepper, then put the breadcrumbs on another plate. Dip each chicken breast into the flour, then the egg, then the breadcrumbs so they are all evenly coated. Make sure they are well coated especially near the incision.

Heat the remaining butter and the sunflower oil in a shallow frying pan on a medium setting. Gently cook the chicken breasts on all sides until golden brown, then transfer them to an ovenproof dish and cook for 10 to 12 minutes depending on the size of the breasts, or until the juices run clear.

Try using chopped fresh coriander instead of parsley for an eastern flavour.

Quick Lamb Biryani

Preparation time: 10 minutes | Cooking time: 40 minutes | Serves: 4

The most memorable biryani we ever had was from the A1 Biryani House in Rameswaram, right at the southern tip of India. Not the most salubrious of establishments but the flavours were immense. This recipe is a quick and very easy version, ideal for a midweek supper.

240g basmati rice

4 large ripe tomatoes

4 tablespoons Hawkshead Relish Hot Garlic Pickle

Olive oil

2 sliced medium onions

Salt and pepper

500g lamb mince

200g frozen peas

100g spinach

300g plain yoghurt

10g chopped mint leaves

10g chopped coriander leaves

1 small finely chopped red onion

1 jar of Hawkshead Relish Mango Chutney

Cook the rice in salted water. Meanwhile, chop the tomatoes into small cubes and crush the Hot Garlic Pickle to a paste.

Heat a little olive oil in a large pan, then add the sliced onion and cook until soft. Add the garlic paste and seasoning, then add the minced lamb and cook until browned. Add the tomatoes, stir and cook for around 10 minutes until the lamb is fully cooked.

Add the peas and spinach and a little water or chicken stock if required. Add the cooked rice and stir through, mixing everything well.

Make a raita using the yoghurt, some of the chopped mint and coriander leaves and the red onion.

Sprinkle the biriyani with chopped coriander and mint, then serve with flatbread, raita and Mango Chutney.

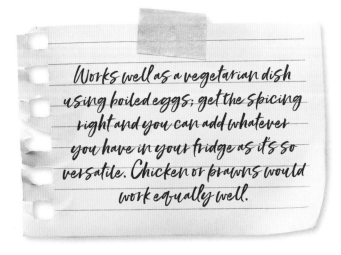

Works well as a vegetarian dish using boiled eggs; get the spicing right and you can add whatever you have in your fridge as it's so versatile. Chicken or prawns would work equally well.

Indian Paneer & Peas

Preparation time: 15 minutes | Cooking time: 25-30 minutes | Serves: 4

We have travelled around India regularly over the last 30 years and this recipe is one that I make at home to remind me of the heat and vibrancy that India offers. It's not too spicy, and I sometimes add little cauliflower florets and small cubes of potato for a change.

2 tablespoons Hawkshead Relish Hot Garlic Pickle

1 teaspoon dried cumin seeds

Splash of vegetable oil

1 cubed block of paneer cheese

1 teaspoon ground turmeric

1 teaspoon chilli flakes

1 teaspoon garam masala

1 sliced onion

1 tin of chopped tomatoes

200g frozen peas

100g baby spinach

To serve

Fresh chopped coriander

Hawkshead Relish Mango Chutney

Crush or chop the Hot Garlic Pickle into a paste. In a dry frying pan over a medium heat, toast the cumin seeds until fragrant, then add a little vegetable oil and the cubed paneer. Cook until the paneer is coloured on all sides then remove the cheese and cumin from the pan and toast the remaining spices for 1 to 2 minutes.

Add a little more oil and the Hot Garlic Pickle to the pan along with the sliced onion. Cook until soft and well coated in the mixture, then add the tomatoes and continue to cook for a couple of minutes until piping hot.

Return the cheese and cumin to the pan along with the frozen peas and spinach and let it simmer until the peas are just hot.

Serve with fresh coriander and our Mango Chutney.

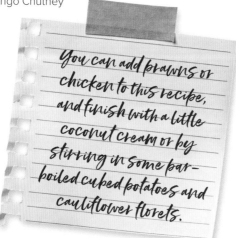

You can add prawns or chicken to this recipe, and finish with a little coconut cream or by stirring in some par-boiled cubed potatoes and cauliflower florets.

Moroccan Lamb Tagine

Preparation time: 15 minutes | Cooking time: 1 hour 30 minutes | Serves: 4

Travel and food is what we love most. This dish is one we often make at home, sometimes using boned chicken thighs instead of lamb. You can make this in a slow cooker and come home to the fragrant scent of spices, then if there's any left, add some stock and make it into a fabulous soup.

45g butter

Dash of vegetable oil

2 tablespoons Hawkshead Relish Hot Garlic Pickle

2 teaspoons ground cumin

1 teaspoon paprika

1 teaspoon cinnamon

550g diced lamb

400g tin of chopped tomatoes

4 large chopped tomatoes

1 large sliced onion

2 diced carrots

Salt and pepper

200ml lamb or chicken stock

400g tin of chickpeas

115g dried apricots

1 tablespoon Hawkshead Relish Mango Chutney

To serve

Couscous

1 lemon

Fresh coriander

Fresh mint

Preheat the oven to 180°c and melt the butter in a large pot with a little vegetable oil. Crush the Hot Garlic Pickle to a paste and add this to the pot along with the spices, followed by the lamb. Stir well to coat the meat in the spices.

Add the tinned and fresh tomatoes, onion and carrots then season with salt and pepper. Add the stock and bring to a boil, then cover and place in the oven to cook for around 1 hour.

Add the chickpeas, apricots and Mango Chutney with a little more stock or water if required, then return the tagine to the oven for a further 15 to 20 minutes.

Meanwhile prepare the couscous, flavouring it with a little lemon zest and chopped herbs.

Serve the tagine with the couscous and a wedge of lemon, then scatter more fresh coriander and mint leaves over the top.

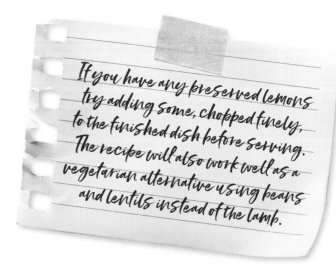

If you have any preserved lemons try adding some, chopped finely, to the finished dish before serving. The recipe will also work well as a vegetarian alternative using beans and lentils instead of the lamb.

Tasty Turmeric Prawns

Preparation time: 10 minutes | Cooking time: 10 minutes | Serves: 4

These are so quick and simple to make and a real favourite. I am always being asked to make some for guests and family to nibble on before dinner or at a summer barbecue. You could use scallops instead or a combination of both for a starter dish.

½ teaspoon chilli powder

¼ teaspoon turmeric powder

Pinch of salt

200g large raw shelled prawns

Vegetable oil

1 heaped tablespoon Hawkshead Relish Hot Garlic Pickle

Chopped fresh coriander

Wedge of fresh lime

Make a marinade using the chilli powder, turmeric and salt. Coat the prawns and leave for at least 30 minutes, longer if you can, covered in the fridge.

Put a little vegetable oil in a pan, chop or blend the Hot Garlic Pickle then cook for about 1 minute. Once hot, add the marinated prawns and stir as they cook in the sauce, making sure they get well coated. Depending on the size of the prawns, they will only take 1 or 2 minutes at the most to cook, turning from grey to pink when ready.

To serve

Sprinkle the prawns with fresh coriander and squeeze over the juice from a wedge of lime then serve hot or cold.

They are great on skewers for the barbecue as well; once you have marinated the prawns grill them on the barbecue for 1 minute, brush with Hot Garlic Pickle, turn, brush again and grill for 1 more minute so they are cooked and flavoured on all sides.

You can use this spice mix for chicken wings as well or Indian paneer – adjust the cooking time and serve with Mango Chutney.

Mango Chutney

Most of us think of Mango Chutney as very sweet, slightly green coloured, sticky goo... but this version will be a revelation to you!

On one of our winter trips to India, we encountered a chutney that had all of the familiar flavours you would expect in a Mango Chutney but was made in an entirely different way, more like a salsa, to be eaten fresh on the day it was made.

As you might expect, Mark busily scribbled down all the details he could get in his trusty notebook and when he got back to the UK, he set about making a version that would last in a jar but would keep the same vibrancy and citrus finish.

I'm pleased to say the result was a magnificent success and has become one of our favourite condiments! Our team love it too, especially as they're partial to a curry and think it's the perfect palate cleanser, but none of us can get enough; it goes on everything and I mean everything!

A certain very well-known two Michelin-starred chef recently told us that this was the best Mango Chutney he had ever had. I guess you can't argue with feedback like that!

Our Mango Chutney recipe includes spices that we roast whole and grind just as we need them, so they are as fresh and pungent as they can be, plus a little chilli so there is warmth but not a fiery heat. It's meant to be an accompaniment after all, but still contains complex layers of flavour that come through to work on your palate, rounded off with a final twist of lemon and lime, leaving you ready for more.

EMBELLISH
WITH RELISH
Mango
chutney
HAWKSHEAD Relish COMPANY

Spiced Lamb Flatbreads

Preparation time: 30 minutes | Cooking time: 12-15 minutes | Serves: 4

As the lamb steaks become coated in the spices, the smell as they roast will fill your home with wonderful eastern aromas. You can serve these with couscous or rice and drizzle the dressing over.

For the lamb

500g lamb leg steaks

1 tablespoon olive oil

1 finely chopped small onion

1 teaspoon dried chilli flakes

Juice of 1 lemon

Salt and pepper

1 teaspoon cumin seeds

For the dressing

175ml plain yoghurt

2 teaspoons Hawkshead Relish Mango Chutney

1 small deseeded and finely chopped chilli

Zest of 1 lemon

Pinch of salt

To serve

4 flatbreads or pitta breads

Pinch of paprika

Salad leaves

Pomegranate seeds

For the lamb

Massage the lamb with the olive oil, onion, chilli flakes, lemon juice, salt and pepper then leave to marinate for as long as you can (a minimum of 30 minutes).

Meanwhile, toast the cumin seeds in a dry frying pan until they start to colour, then grind them to a powder using a pestle and mortar.

Heat a griddle pan or heavy-based frying pan until very hot, add the marinated lamb steaks and cook for a few minutes on each side until nicely browned all over. Spoon the remaining marinade over the meat then remove from the heat to rest. After a couple of minutes, slice the steaks into thin strips.

For the dressing

Mix all the ingredients for the dressing together then cover and refrigerate until needed.

To serve

Warm the flatbreads. Add the lamb, sprinkle with paprika and the toasted cumin powder then drizzle with the dressing. Serve with a fresh green salad dotted with pomegranate seeds.

To warm the flatbreads, either pop in a microwave for 10 seconds or place in a hot dry frying pan for a few seconds on each side so they soften and start to colour but don't burn.

Fruity Pork & Mango Bake

Preparation time: 15 minutes | Cooking time: 40-50 minutes | Serves: 4

Family suppers baked in one dish in the oven are a great way to simplify the meal as well as the clearing up afterwards! You could make this dish in the slow cooker, and adapt it to use whatever vegetables you have in, or use apples instead of pears; it's a versatile recipe.

2 tablespoons olive oil

2 roughly chopped onions

4 peeled and finely chopped cloves of garlic

1 teaspoon coriander seeds

1 teaspoon paprika

2 tablespoons Hawkshead Relish Mango Chutney

1 tablespoon tomato purée

1 deseeded and finely chopped red chilli

200ml white wine

Knob of butter

4 pork chops

1 peeled, cored and cubed pear

300ml stock (chicken or vegetable)

Salt and pepper

Preheat the oven to 180°c. Add a little oil to a large pan and fry off the onions until they are soft, then add the garlic and cook, being careful not to let anything colour and burn. Add the coriander seeds, paprika, Mango Chutney, tomato purée, chilli and wine. Bring the mixture to a simmer and then transfer to an ovenproof dish ready for the pork.

In a separate pan, heat a knob of butter and a little olive oil then gently fry the chops until coloured on all sides. Lay them in the oven dish with the cubed pear and pour over the stock. Season well with salt and pepper.

Cook in the preheated oven for approximately 30 to 40 minutes, depending on the thickness of the pork chops. They should be tender and slightly pink when ready.

Serve with green beans and cumin-infused rice with extra Mango Chutney on the side.

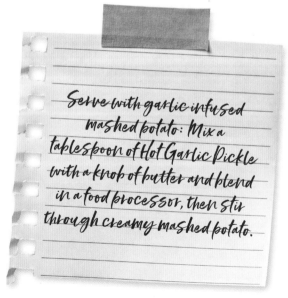

Serve with garlic-infused mashed potato: Mix a tablespoon of Hot Garlic Pickle with a knob of butter and blend in a food processor, then stir through creamy mashed potato.

Buttermilk Fried Chicken Sandwich

Preparation Time: 10-15 minutes | Cooking time: 10 minutes | Serves: 4

While you don't have to soak the chicken in buttermilk, it does make the meat incredibly soft and tender so give it a go if you can. This dish is a real crowd pleaser for all the family; served alongside a salad or in a sandwich as we have done, it's a winner.

4 skinned chicken breasts

350ml buttermilk

150g plain flour

2 teaspoons dried oregano

2 teaspoons paprika

2 teaspoons onion powder

1 teaspoon garlic powder

1½ teaspoons cayenne pepper

Salt and pepper

Vegetable oil

4 tablespoons mayonnaise

1 tablespoon Hawkshead Relish Mango Chutney

4 crusty rolls

1 red onion

Lettuce leaves

To serve:

Homemade coleslaw

Fries

Lay the chicken breasts between two pieces of cling film and bash with a rolling pin until they are about 2cm in thickness. Place the chicken in a bowl with the buttermilk, cover and chill in the fridge for a minimum of 2 hours.

Mix the dry ingredients together in a bowl.

Drain the chicken and either cut into strips or leave in large pieces as preferred.

Heat the vegetable oil to 175°c while you coat each chicken breast with the seasoned flour mixture. Drop the first one carefully into the oil and cook separately for around 4 to 5 minutes or until golden brown and crispy (the timing will depend on the size of the chicken breasts). Drain on kitchen paper and repeat with the other chicken breasts.

Mix the mayonnaise and Mango Chutney together, slightly toast the rolls under a hot grill and slice the onion into rings.

Coat the base of each roll with the mango mayonnaise, top with lettuce, onion and a piece of fried chicken then finish with another spoonful of the mayo. Add the top half of the roll and serve with homemade coleslaw and fries.

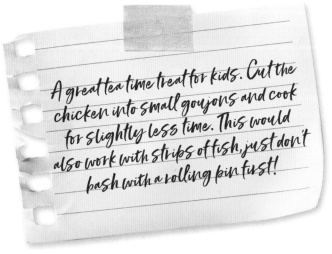

A great tea time treat for kids. Cut the chicken into small goujons and cook for slightly less time. This would also work with strips of fish, just don't bash with a rolling pin first!

Thai Mango Prawn Noodles

Preparation time: 15-20 minutes | Cooking time: 15 minutes | Serves: 4

Thai cuisine is notable for the fragrant flavours of ginger, garlic and lemongrass so this recipe evokes many happy memories of Thailand for me. Devised with local chef Martin Frickel, it's a lovely mix of fruitiness and spice, finished with the vibrant green coriander leaves.

200g dried rice noodles

1 small carrot

Juice and zest of 1 lime

2 tablespoons Hawkshead Relish Mango Chutney

1 tablespoon light soy sauce

1½ tablespoons fish sauce

1 tablespoon Thai red chilli paste

1 finely chopped red chilli

1 tablespoon vegetable oil

1 bunch of chopped spring onions

50g grated fresh ginger

3 crushed cloves of garlic

100g sugar snap peas

350g large raw cleaned and shelled tiger prawns

150g fresh beansprouts

To serve

Lime wedges

Crushed roasted peanuts

Hawkshead Relish Mango Chutney

Put the noodles in a bowl and pour boiling water over them to soak for a few minutes. Create carrot ribbons using a vegetable peeler.

To make the sauce, mix together the lime juice and zest, Mango Chutney, soy sauce, fish sauce and chilli paste. Add three quarters of the chopped chilli and six tablespoons of water then mix well.

Heat the vegetable oil in a large frying pan or wok. When hot, stir in the spring onion, ginger and garlic, then the sugar snap peas and carrot ribbons. Once everything is coated, add the prawns and most of the beansprouts along with the sauce. Cook until the prawns turn pink; it will only take a couple of minutes so be careful not to overcook them.

Drain the soaked noodles, add them to the pan and quickly stir through. Serve with lime wedges, crushed roasted peanuts, the rest of the chopped chilli, a handful of fresh beansprouts and a little more Mango Chutney.

You can turn the heat up to taste with more chilli if you wish; it's all down to personal preference.

Try serving inside a thin egg omelette for a street food feel. Make one omelette per person as thin as you can, fill one side with the prawn noodles and flip over to cover then serve with Mango Chutney and a sprinkling of coriander leaves.

Keralan Mango Chicken

Preparation time: 25 minutes | Cooking time: 30-40 minutes | Serves: 4

Kerala in southern India is a place we love and return to often. We buy spices from the farms in the Cardamom Hills and explore the hill stations and backwaters. Coconut is the staple in just about every Keralan dish, and we have been known to take our own Mango Chutney to India!

4 skinned chicken breasts

2 small bananas

4 tablespoons Hawkshead Relish Mango Chutney

12 slices of streaky smoked bacon

Freshly ground black pepper

Olive oil

For the raita

300g plain yoghurt

1 finely diced small red onion

¼ peeled and finely diced cucumber

1 teaspoon Hawkshead Relish Mango Chutney

½ chopped red chilli

1 teaspoon chopped mint

1 teaspoon chopped coriander

Salt and pepper

For the rice

300g basmati rice

400ml coconut milk

10g cumin seeds

Chopped fresh coriander leaves

Preheat the oven to 200°c. With a sharp knife, make an incision in the top edge of the thicker part of the chicken breast. Use the knife to open up a pouch inside the chicken, being careful not to break through the flesh. Mash the banana and Mango Chutney together and use a piping bag to squeeze the mixture into the cavity. Seal with a cocktail stick then wrap the chicken breast in two slices of the streaky bacon and season with black pepper. Repeat with each breast then place them in a greased oven dish and drizzle over a little olive oil.

Cook in the hot oven for 20 to 25 minutes depending on the size of the chicken breasts. The juices should run clear when it is cooked through. Make the raita and rice while the chicken is cooking.

For the raita

Combine all the ingredients thoroughly and season with salt and pepper to taste.

For the rice

Cook the rice in the coconut milk, adding a little extra water only if needed. Bring to the boil, reduce the heat and let it simmer gently for about 15 minutes, allowing the rice to absorb all the liquid. Once it is cooked, let it stand for a few minutes then fluff with a fork.

In a dry frying pan toast the cumin seeds until they start to change colour, then mix through the rice just before serving. Sprinkle the rice with fresh coriander and serve with the chicken breasts and raita.

Make a quick and easy sauce to serve with this dish using a can of creamed coconut and a tablespoon of Mango Chutney; mix together in a saucepan and heat gently until warm but not allowing it to boil. Season and serve with the chicken.

Chilli Jam

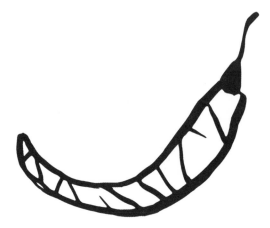

We designed our Chilli Jam to be hot and sweet, but with chillies that you can taste rather than ones that blast your taste buds into next week.

It's one of those condiments that you'll be reaching for time and time again. Once you start adding it to dishes, whether they're hearty savouries or sweet treats, you won't stop... it adds a layer of flavour and just a little heat that you will love!

Here are a few recipe ideas to get you started:

- Stir into sauces, gravies or stir fries for a quick chilli kick

- Use to pep up your Bolognese or chilli con carne

- Whisk with a little vinegar and oil to make yourself a spicy dressing

- Add a teaspoon to a rich hot chocolate on a frosty day

- Sneak some into a chocolate cake mix for a touch of background heat

- Drizzle over ice cream for a hot/cold sensation

- Make a quick marinade for barbecued meat and fish with crushed ginger, garlic and lemon juice

- Fold through homemade coleslaw

- Enhance minestrone soup with a swirl before serving

Go on: be bold and adventurous with our Chilli Jam! Add a little, have a taste and then add a bit more if you want it hotter... you can always add a little more as you go along, but do remember you can't take it out once it's in.

EMBELLISH
WITH RELISH
Chilli
jam
HAWKSHEAD Relish COMPANY

Goat's Cheese & Chilli Tarts

Preparation time: 10 minutes | Cooking time: 20 minutes | Serves: 4

Made as little tartlets, these are ideal for party snacks or light lunches. They are quick and easy to prepare, and if you don't like goat's cheese you can use something like a tasty Lancashire cheese or camembert instead. You could make one large tart instead of individual ones if preferred.

150g ready-rolled puff pastry

2 tablespoons Hawkshead Relish Chilli Jam

150g log of goat's cheese

100g cherry tomatoes on the vine

2 tablespoons olive oil

Salt and pepper

Fresh basil leaves

Preheat the oven to 180°c and line two baking trays.

Cut the pastry into four rounds and prick each one with a fork. Transfer them to a lined tray. Add a teaspoon of Chilli Jam to each one and top with a slice or two of goat's cheese to cover the jam.

Place the tomatoes on a separate baking tray and drizzle with a little olive oil then season with salt and pepper.

Place both trays in the oven for 15 to 20 minutes until the cheese is soft and browned on the top and the tomatoes are hot.

Place a couple of tomatoes on the top of each tart, drizzle with a little more olive oil and add a basil leaf or two as a finishing touch.

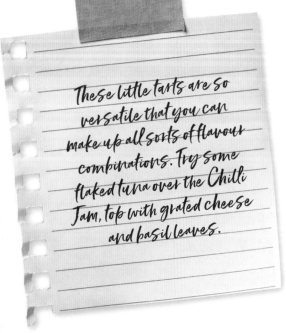

These little tarts are so versatile that you can make up all sorts of flavour combinations. Try some flaked tuna over the Chilli Jam, top with grated cheese and basil leaves.

Sticky Chilli Chicken

Preparation time: 20 minutes | Cooking time: 40 minutes | Serves: 4

We came across this dish a few years ago while travelling in Vietnam, and it has quickly become a family favourite. It's quick and easy to make and you can use pork, prawns or fish instead of the chicken. You could also skewer the chicken pieces and heat the sauce to serve separately.

900g boneless skinned chicken thighs

2 tablespoons vegetable oil

For the marinade

1 teaspoon Hawkshead Relish Chilli Jam

2 tablespoons fish sauce

1 finely chopped onion

2 finely chopped cloves of garlic

Freshly ground black pepper

1 finely chopped green chilli

10g grated fresh ginger

For the sauce

100g brown sugar

2 tablespoons Hawkshead Relish Chilli Jam

4 teaspoons fish sauce

750ml hot chicken stock

1 finely chopped chilli

40g finely chopped fresh ginger

1 teaspoon ground cinnamon

1 teaspoon black peppercorns

1 teaspoon lime juice

To serve

2½cm ginger

2 spring onions

Fresh coriander

Extra chilli (optional)

For the marinade

Chop the chicken into 5cm pieces. Combine all the marinade ingredients in a bowl, add the chicken, mix well, cover and leave in the fridge for around 1 hour to marinate.

For the sauce

Put the sugar in a pan and heat gently until it has melted without allowing it to burn. Turn up the heat and stir until the liquid sugar turns a darker colour, then remove from the heat and add the Chilli Jam and fish sauce. Be careful as it can bubble up and burn you.

Add 500ml of the stock, followed by the chilli, ginger, cinnamon, black peppercorns and lime juice.

Heat the vegetable oil in a frying pan, then when the oil is hot and almost at smoking point add the marinated chicken pieces and stir constantly to avoid them sticking and burning. Allow to brown for a couple of minutes then use the rest of the stock to deglaze the pan and create a caramelised sauce. Cook this out until the liquid has reduced by a quarter.

Serve with steamed rice and top with thinly sliced ginger and spring onions, fresh coriander, and more chopped chilli if you like the extra heat.

Sprinkle with toasted sesame seeds to finish. Also great in flatbreads wrapped up with chopped lettuce, chopped spring onion, chopped red chilli or Chilli Jam and extra chopped coriander leaves.

Spanish Chicken & Chorizo

Preparation time: 25 minutes | Cooking time: 45-60 minutes | Serves: 4

My mother's family come from Las Palmas in Spain, so I have always loved cooking anything that evokes the flavours and colours of her home country. We have been making this dish for more years than I care to think about; it's a great family meal packed with flavour and sunshine.

12 chicken thighs

4 tablespoons olive oil

4 cloves of garlic

2 teaspoons paprika

2 sprigs of rosemary

Salt and pepper

3 large sweet potatoes

140g sliced cooking chorizo

200g mini sweet peppers

2 quartered red onions

2 tablespoons Hawkshead Relish Chilli Jam

Juice of 2 oranges

100g pitted Kalamata olives

220g cherry tomatoes on the vine

60g mini pickled peppers

10g fresh basil

Preheat the oven to 180°c.

Mix the chicken thighs with the oil, garlic, paprika, rosemary, salt and pepper then leave them to marinate for 10 to 15 minutes.

Peel and dice the sweet potatoes then add them to the chicken along with the chorizo, peppers and red onion. Transfer the mixture to a large roasting tray with the chicken skin side up, and place into the preheated oven for 25 minutes.

Meanwhile, combine the Chilli Jam and orange juice. When the initial cooking time is up, pour this over the chicken and add the olives, cherry tomatoes and pickled peppers to the roasting tray. Return to the oven for another 15 to 20 minutes, allowing the chicken skin to crisp up. Finish with torn basil leaves scattered over the top, and serve with a fresh rocket salad.

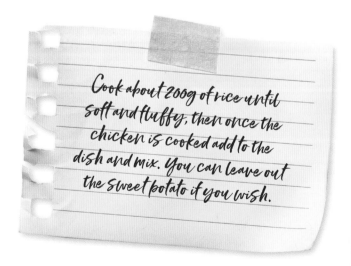

Cook about 200g of rice until soft and fluffy, then once the chicken is cooked add to the dish and mix. You can leave out the sweet potato if you wish.

Thai Chilli Fishcakes

Preparation time: 15 minutes | Cooking time: 10-15 minutes | Serves: 4

On the years we don't travel to India, we invariably head off east. The flavours of Thailand, Laos, Vietnam and Cambodia are so vibrant and delicious while not always so spicy. These fishcakes give you a hint of the heat, but you can add more chilli if that's your thing!

6 fresh kaffir lime leaves

1 finely chopped stalk of lemongrass

1 teaspoon fish sauce

Small bunch of fresh coriander

1 tablespoon Hawkshead Relish Chilli Jam

1 tablespoon Thai curry paste

3 finely chopped spring onions

75g fresh breadcrumbs

450g crabmeat

Flour

Olive oil

Butter

Put all the ingredients except the crabmeat, flour, oil and butter into a food processor and blitz.

Fold in the crabmeat and then check the seasoning, adding more if required.

Form the mixture into small patties, dust with a little flour and then fry each one in butter and oil on a medium heat for 3 to 4 minutes on each side.

Make into little bon bons and cook to serve as a starter or light lunch with a crisp salad and a Chilli Jam dressing. Mix equal amounts of Chilli Jam with rice wine vinegar to dip the bon bons in.

I have also used this mix to make a crust for a salmon steak; spread it over the top and bake in the oven until the salmon is just cooked through. Served with stir fried vegetables and rice.

Tex-Mex Cottage Pie

Preparation time: 20 minutes | Cooking time: 45 minutes | Serves: 4

Get the beers in and invite a crowd; a big bowl of spicy cottage pie with crunchy corn chips and melted cheese topping is just crying out for party. Try using chicken strips and avocado instead of mince for an alternative.

2 sweet potatoes

Olive oil

2 cubed green peppers

2 cubed carrots

500g beef mince

2 sliced onions

2 tablespoons Hawkshead Relish Chilli Jam

2 beef stock cubes

2 x 400g tins of chopped tomatoes

1 tablespoon tomato purée

Salt and pepper

340g tin of sweetcorn

150g plain corn chips

400g grated cheddar cheese

150ml sour cream

1 avocado

4 or 5 chopped chives

1 fresh lime

Preheat the oven to 200°c. Peel and chop the sweet potatoes into 2cm cubes, spread out on a greased oven tray and bake for 20 minutes until golden brown.

Heat a little olive oil in a frying pan, add the pepper and carrot, cook for 5 minutes, remove and set aside. Add a little more oil to the pan and add the beef mince. Cook for 4 to 5 minutes or until browned all over.

When the meat is lightly browned, add the onion and cook until softened, then add the Chilli Jam, stock cubes, chopped tomatoes and tomato purée. Season with salt and pepper.

Drain the sweetcorn then add it to the pan along with the peppers and carrots. Simmer until the sauce has reduced and thickened.

Transfer the pie filling into an ovenproof dish, top with the sweet potato and corn chips, then sprinkle a layer of cheese over the top.

Bake in the oven for around 10 to 15 minutes until the cheese has all melted.

Serve with sour cream, cubed fresh avocado, a sprinkling of fresh chives and a wedge of lime.

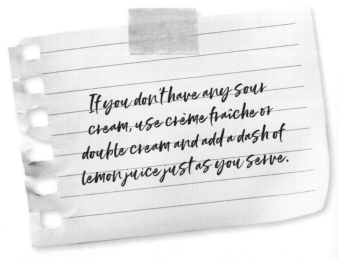

If you don't have any sour cream, use crème fraîche or double cream and add a dash of lemon juice just as you serve.

Chilli Rocky Road

Preparation time: 10 minutes plus 1 hour chilling | Cooking time: 15 minutes | Serves: 4

These beauties are far too delicious for their own good. The high cocoa content of the chocolate keeps them from being too sickly, and the Chilli Jam gives background warmth without packing a punch, but if you'd like them hotter just add a little more chilli!

50g peanuts

50g shelled pistachios

250g 70% dark chocolate

50g dried apricots

50g dried cherries

50g marshmallows

2 tablespoons pumpkin seeds

2 tablespoons Hawkshead Relish Chilli Jam

Pinch of sea salt

Preheat the oven to 180°c. Lightly grease and line an 8 by 20cm loaf tin with non-stick greaseproof paper.

Scatter the nuts on a baking tray and cook until golden for 6 minutes, then allow to cool.

Gently melt the chocolate over a pan of boiling water. Allow to cool slightly before folding in all the remaining ingredients except the sea salt, including the nuts, and mix thoroughly. If you are using mini marshmallows they can go straight in, but chop large ones up beforehand.

Pour into the loaf tin, press down into the corners then sprinkle with sea salt. Leave to set in the fridge for at least 1 hour, then cut into squares or fingers as you prefer.

Keep in an airtight container for as long as they last! Great for dipping in hot chocolate on a crisp, cold winter's day.

Black Garlic Ketchup

How long have you got?

This unique ketchup was completely dreamt up by Mark, and what a sensation it's been, winning lots of awards (including Innovation and Product of the Year) since we launched it in 2017.

By late 2018 it had even knocked Westmorland Chutney off our top seller spot, and it certainly isn't showing signs of budging anytime soon...

It all started when I went to Japan on a trade trip hosted by the British Embassy. I picked up a jar of black garlic cloves because I knew Mark would be fascinated by them, especially as I'd never come across them before.

I was right, he loved them, but they sat in our fridge for months! We loved their flavour but as whole cloves they were just a bit tricky to use in dishes. Then Mark had a bit of a brainwave and came up with the idea of creating a Black Garlic Ketchup. Traditionally, ketchups are indicatively sweet, so it seemed the perfect medium.

So, what is black garlic?

Black garlic is simply normal garlic, which is cooked in whole bulbs for around 50 days. Yes, that is days not hours! On a low heat and with a high humidity, a bit like when you cook onions on a low heat, they caramelise over time. The enzymes which create the heat and harsh garlic flavour you associate with the raw bulb turn to sugar, and they turn black, sticky and sweet.

At this stage we blend them with balsamic vinegar for added depth of flavour, along with tomatoes and selected spices. The end result is a deliciously rich and sweet-edged ketchup that's great with everything from eggs to fish and meat. Simply serve with burgers or steaks, add to risottos or casseroles, or use to pep up your gravy and soups.

It's early days but we haven't yet found anything it doesn't go with!

THE ORIGINAL

Black
Garlic
ketchup

HAWKSHEAD *Relish* COMPANY

Baked Cod & Tomatoes

Preparation time: 10 minutes | Cooking time: 25 minutes | Serves: 4

The sweetness of black garlic is fantastic with fish and tomatoes. You can use hake, sea bass, haddock or salmon instead of cod for this recipe – just ask your fishmonger to skin and debone the fish for you – which is quick and easy to prepare.

1 finely diced small onion

200g halved cherry tomatoes

Dash of olive oil

Salt and pepper

4 x 120g skinned cod loins

4 tablespoons Hawkshead Relish Black Garlic Ketchup

2 slices of white bread

15g chopped flat leaf parsley

2 large chopped cloves of garlic

Zest of 1 lemon

For the white bean salad

340g tin of cannellini beans

1 small finely chopped red onion

1 teaspoon chopped mint

2 tablespoons olive oil

1 tablespoon sherry vinegar

Salt and pepper

Heat the oven to 180°c. Sauté the onion and tomatoes in a frying pan with a little olive oil to soften them, then transfer to an ovenproof dish. Season with salt and pepper and drizzle over a little more olive oil, then place in the oven for 8 minutes.

Place the fish on top of the tomato mix and top each piece with a spoonful of Black Garlic Ketchup. Remove the crusts from the bread and whizz or tear into breadcrumbs. Mix these with the parsley, garlic, lemon zest, and seasoning. Sprinkle the crumb on top of the fish.

Bake in the oven for around 10 to 14 minutes, depending on the thickness of the fish, so it's just cooked through. Meanwhile, make the accompaniment.

For the white bean salad

Drain and rinse the cannellini beans, then mix all the ingredients together.

Serve the salad on the side with the crumbed fish and tomato base.

Serve with chargrilled baby gem lettuce; simply slice a whole baby gem in half lengthways, and sear in a hot grill pan or frying pan with a little olive oil until blackened and just warmed through.

Black Garlic Peppered Salmon

Preparation time: 10 minutes | Cooking time: 15 minutes | Serves: 4

Using the crushed black peppercorns with the sweet Black Garlic Ketchup gives this recipe a heat and texture that works so well with the salmon. It looks stunning and is so quick and easy to prepare.

4 x 220g salmon fillets

2 tablespoons mixed whole peppercorns

2 tablespoons Hawkshead Relish Black Garlic Ketchup

25ml olive oil

Seasoned plain flour

Long grain and wild rice

Preheat the oven to 180°c.

Crush the peppercorns roughly using a pestle and mortar or a rolling pin, mix the Black Garlic Ketchup with a little olive oil and dust each piece of fish in the seasoned flour.

In a frying pan, heat a little olive oil and shallow fry the fish one or two at a time for about 3 minutes on each side. Spoon over the Black Garlic Ketchup mix then sprinkle the crushed peppercorns over the top. Finish in the oven for 5 minutes until the salmon is just cooked through.

Serve with long grain and wild rice, with any remaining sauce spooned over the fish.

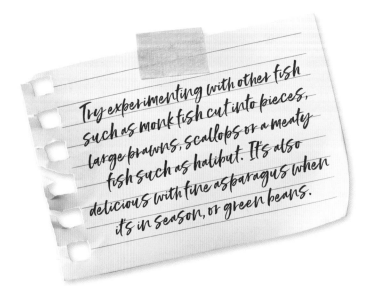

Try experimenting with other fish such as monk fish cut into pieces, large prawns, scallops or a meaty fish such as halibut. It's also delicious with fine asparagus when it's in season, or green beans.

Bulgarian Black Chicken

Preparation time: 15-20 minutes | Cooking time: 45-50 minutes | Serves: 4

A very old family favourite. In this one pot dish, the potatoes are quite al dente and the vinegar is quite prominent, but everything is balanced by the Black Garlic Ketchup.

1kg potatoes

8 skin-on chicken thighs

4 fresh tomatoes, diced

2 tablespoons olive oil

Pinch of paprika

1 chopped onion

2 finely chopped cloves of garlic

1 chicken stock cube

Salt and pepper

For the sauce

400g tin of chopped tomatoes

3 tablespoons red wine vinegar

2 tablespoons Hawkshead Relish Black Garlic Ketchup

1 tablespoon tomato purée

Juice of 1 lemon

Sprig of fresh rosemary

3 tablespoons chopped parsley

Heat the oven to 180°c and peel the potatoes then chop them into 3 to 4cm cubes.

Place the chicken, fresh tomatoes and potatoes in an ovenproof dish. Brush all over with olive oil and dust with paprika.

In a frying pan, gently cook the onion and garlic in olive oil to soften them, then add the sauce ingredients and stir to warm through.

Pour the sauce over the chicken, tomatoes and potato then sprinkle over the chicken stock cube and season with salt and pepper.

Cover and bake in the oven for 20 minutes, then remove the cover and baste the chicken with the sauce, adding a little water if required. Return to the oven for a further 30 minutes until everything is cooked through. Serve with chopped parsley, sour cream and flatbread.

Serve with sour cream or crème fraîche mixed through with chopped parsley.

Mexican Ham & Egg Brunch

Preparation time: 30 minutes | Cooking time: 25-30 minutes | Serves: 4

A great way to use up leftover cooked ham, these pots make a fabulous lunch dish or an irresistible brunch, best served with a crunchy ciabatta roll. The flavour is reminiscent of huevos rancheros, and black garlic with eggs is a match made in heaven.

Olive oil

100g diced chorizo

2 tablespoons Hawkshead Relish Black Garlic Ketchup

325g tin of sweetcorn

200g tin of mixed beans

400g tin of cherry tomatoes

2 teaspoons Hawkshead Relish Worcester Sauce

400g shredded cooked ham

4 eggs

Fresh coriander

Pinch of cayenne pepper

Black pepper

Preheat the oven to 180°c and heat a little olive oil in a pan. Add the chorizo and cook for a few minutes, then add the Black Garlic Ketchup and allow it to warm through.

Drain the sweetcorn and mixed beans then add them to the pan along with the tomatoes and Worcester Sauce. Cook for 8 to 10 minutes then fold in the ham.

Transfer the mixture into an ovenproof dish and gently break the eggs on top. Place into the oven and bake for 10 to 15 minutes so that the egg is just cooked. You can adjust the time depending on how runny you like your eggs.

Sprinkle with coriander, cayenne pepper and freshly ground pepper.

Nearly all breakfast dishes in Mexico feature avocado, either sliced, diced or crushed, so serve this with avocado prepared as you prefer and a wedge of lime.

Monday Night Supper

Preparation time: 10 minutes | Cooking time: 25 minutes | Serves: 4

Assuming you've had a roast on Sunday and have some leftovers, this is our go-to dish for using up the cooked meat and vegetables. It's quick and easy to prepare, and after a long day back at work it's a real comfort food triumph. Think of this recipe as more of a guide, and adapt it to your own preferences and leftovers.

500g cooked meat (such as pork, beef or lamb left over from the Sunday roast)

2 large potatoes

Vegetable oil

2 chopped onions

4 chopped rashers of streaky bacon

200g frozen peas or leftover root veg (such as roasted carrots or parsnips)

2 tablespoons Hawkshead Relish Black Garlic Ketchup

1 tablespoon Hawkshead Relish Worcester Sauce

Freshly ground black pepper

4 eggs

Chopped fresh parsley

Cut the meat into 3 to 4cm pieces, then peel the potatoes and cube them roughly the same size.

Add a little oil to a large frying pan and fry the potatoes until they are nicely browned all over. Remove and keep warm on a plate lined with kitchen paper to soak up excess oil. Using the same pan, add a touch more oil and fry the onions until they are soft and translucent, then add the bacon and cook until starting to crisp. Add the cubed meat and the peas or diced root vegetables to warm through, then add the Black Garlic Ketchup and the Hawkshead Relish Worcester Sauce. Season the mixture with freshly ground black pepper. Transfer the potatoes back into the pan and stir gently to ensure they are coated in the sauce.

In a separate pan, fry the eggs and then serve the hash with an egg on top and a sprinkle of chopped parsley for each person.

If you haven't got enough leftover meat from the Sunday roast, you can always add some sausages instead; just make sure they are cooked through before adding the sauces.

Pasta Pronto

Preparation time: 5-10 minutes | Cooking time: 15 minutes | Serves: 4

Assuming you have some dried pasta in the cupboard, this recipe is meant to be a base for a quick supper dish. You can add bacon lardons, a drained pot of clams – fresh ones would be even better if you can get them – or keep it vegetarian with some asparagus spears.

Olive oil

2 finely chopped cloves of garlic

1 teaspoon Hawkshead Relish Chilli Jam

1 tablespoon Hawkshead Relish Black Garlic Ketchup

1 tablespoon tomato purée

400g tin of chopped tomatoes

180g pitted, drained and chopped olives

1 heaped tablespoon capers

2 anchovy fillets

1 teaspoon dried basil

Salt and pepper

500g pasta, preferably spaghetti

To serve

Fresh basil

Parmesan

Heat a little oil in a saucepan, add the chopped garlic and cook until golden. Add the rest of the ingredients, stir and season with salt and pepper.

Turn the heat down and simmer the sauce without a lid for around 30 minutes until thickened. Cook and drain the pasta then add it to the sauce and mix well to coat.

Serve with fresh basil leaves and grated Parmesan.

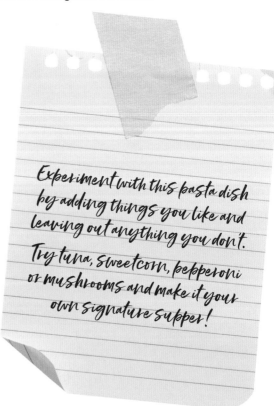

Experiment with this pasta dish by adding things you like and leaving out anything you don't. Try tuna, sweetcorn, pepperoni or mushrooms and make it your own signature supper!

Wing Dings

Preparation time: 10-15 minutes | Cooking time: 1 hour | Serves: 4

On a fabulous holiday in Florida many years ago, we came across these spicy wings, although they were a lot hotter there. We came home and adapted the recipe so that you can have some feeling left in your lips afterwards! But if you like yours hot, be our guest and add more chilli.

2.3kg chicken wings

3 teaspoons paprika

Salt and pepper

100ml vegetable oil

100ml Hawkshead Relish Black Garlic Ketchup

50ml tomato ketchup

1 tablespoon crushed garlic

6 tablespoons white wine vinegar

2 tablespoons Hawkshead Relish Worcester Sauce

2 tablespoons Hawkshead Relish Chilli Jam

1 teaspoon Hawkshead Relish Honey Mustard

4 tablespoons melted butter

Preheat the oven to 200°c.

Sprinkle the wings with paprika and season them with salt and pepper, then pour over a little vegetable oil and cook in the oven for 15 minutes.

Mix the rest of the ingredients together in a small saucepan, heat until the mixture reaches boiling point and then remove from the heat.

Place the chicken wings in a shallow ovenproof dish, brush with the sauce and cook in the hot oven for 15 minutes. Turn the wings over and brush them again then cook for another 15 minutes. Take the wings out of the oven, pour the rest of the sauce over them and then put back in the oven for at least 15 more minutes, until the wings have been in the oven for over 1 hour in total.

Serve with rice and salad, or cooled as a picnic dish.

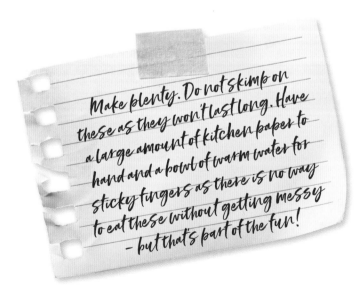

Make plenty. Do not skimp on these as they won't last long. Have a large amount of kitchen paper to hand and a bowl of warm water for sticky fingers as there is no way to eat these without getting messy – but that's part of the fun!

Beetroot & Horseradish Chutney

Our Beetroot & Horseradish Chutney came about following a dinner at home. We were having my mum's famous Lancashire hotpot with some pickled beetroot on the side, as you do...

Mark was intrigued by the flavours on his plate and decided to create a chutney to match. Over the following few weeks, Mark worked on a recipe that combined beetroot with apples, onions, raisins and a hint of horseradish.

Not only does the chutney work with hotpots, it also goes brilliantly with lots of other dishes and ingredients including cottage pie, beef, salmon and smoked mackerel.

It's great in a sandwich too; I remember my mum making me Lancashire cheese and beetroot sandwiches for school trips... by the time I got around to eating the sandwiches the bread would be vibrantly pink and soft but utterly delicious!

Like many of our relishes, Beetroot & Horseradish Chutney is a store cupboard staple; it's one that you can add to all sorts of dishes, including soups and stews, and even discover new and innovative pairings with a little bit of experimentation. But of course, it's also perfect just to have alongside your cheeseboard!

EMBELLISH
WITH RELISH

Beetroot
and
Horseradish
chutney

HAWKSHEAD *Relish* COMPANY

Ham & Beetroot Patties

Preparation time: 20 minutes | Cooking time: 30 minutes | Serves: 4

My mum would make a hash using corned beef, but I love the flavour of these with ham and beetroot so I have adapted this to make little cakes. With a softly poached egg over the top they make for a delicious brunch dish.

400g peeled and chopped potatoes

40g butter

200g shredded leeks

1 teaspoon mustard powder

2 teaspoons chopped parsley

150g shredded ham hock

60g grated cheddar cheese

2 tablespoons Hawkshead Relish Beetroot & Horseradish Chutney

Plain flour

Vegetable oil

To serve

4 eggs

Salad leaves

Asparagus spears

Boil the potatoes in salted water for around 15 minutes until soft. Drain, season and mash well until smooth.

Melt the butter in a pan and add the shredded leeks. Cook over a low heat until the leeks are cooked but not browned.

Add the leeks to the potato along with the mustard powder, parsley, ham and cheese then mix together well. Finally add the Beetroot & Horseradish Chutney and stir gently to combine all the ingredients.

Form the mixture into four equal sized patties and lightly dust with flour.

Heat a little vegetable oil in a frying pan and fry the patties gently on a medium heat for around 5 minutes on each side until golden and crispy. You can start them off on the hob and finish them in the oven if you prefer.

To serve

Top each patty with a lightly poached egg, and serve on a bed of salad leaves or with some gently cooked asparagus spears.

Try making this with some flaked hot smoked salmon instead of the ham.

My Mum's Legendary Lamb Hotpot

Preparation time: 20 minutes | Cooking time: 2 hours 30 minutes | Serves: 4

Growing up in Southport, the annual harvest supper was a big calendar event in the village of Churchtown. Long tables were laid with dishes of hotpot brought from home, and people fought to sit closest to my mum's! It still takes me back when I smell this cooking.

600g lamb neck fillet

Salt and pepper

3 tablespoons olive oil

1 roughly chopped large carrot

1 roughly chopped stick of celery

1 roughly chopped large onion

1 whole horseshoe of Bury black pudding, cut into cubes

1 litre beef or lamb stock

1 tablespoon Hawkshead Relish Worcester Sauce

Fresh thyme

Bay leaves

2 tablespoons Hawkshead Relish Beetroot & Horseradish Chutney

3-4 thinly sliced large Maris Piper potatoes

100g melted butter

Preheat the oven to 180°c. Dice the lamb into 2 to 3cm cubes, then season it with plenty of salt and pepper. Heat the oil in a large frying pan, and when it's hot sear the lamb until brown on all sides.

Using a large ovenproof dish with a lid, layer the base with a handful of chopped vegetables then season with salt and pepper. Add a layer of lamb and the cubed black pudding and then the rest of the vegetables and meat, seasoning as you go. My mum's version was very heavy on the pepper, but season to your own taste.

Heat the stock then add the Worcester Sauce, herbs and chutney to it and allow everything to melt together before pouring the mixture over the vegetables and meat. The liquid should just cover everything.

Place the sliced potatoes in a bowl and mix with the melted butter, season with salt and pepper, then arrange the slices over the top of the hotpot until the dish is covered. Mum used to make them several layers deep so there was enough for everyone. The top ones will be crispy so you'll have to fight for these!

Cover the hotpot with the lid and place in the preheated oven for 30 minutes, then reduce the temperature to 150°c and cook for 1 hour. Remove the lid and allow the potatoes to crisp up and brown for a further 30 minutes.

Allow to rest then serve with more Beetroot & Horseradish Chutney on the side.

I like to also use neck chops in my hotpot. Buy them from your butcher and ask for meaty ones. If you don't like black pudding just leave it out. You can make this dish with a good Cumberland Sausage instead of the lamb, cut in to chunks.

Salmon & Beetroot Bake

Preparation time: 5 minutes | Cooking time: 20 minutes | Serves: 4

Both Anne and Monica from our offices offered a similar suggestion for this dish. I have tried it a few times now at home and it's a keeper! So simple and delicious, and best of all ready in half an hour. The individual parcels make this a great dinner party dish.

4 x 150g salmon fillets

2 tablespoons Hawkshead Relish Beetroot & Horseradish Chutney

2 finely sliced red onions

1-2 teaspoons chopped parsley

1-2 teaspoons chopped dill

Zest of 1 lemon

To Serve

Couscous

Steamed vegetables

Heat the oven to 180°c.

Grease a piece of baking parchment, place the first salmon fillet in the centre and spoon over half a tablespoon of chutney. Top with quarter of the onion, a sprinkle of herbs and a generous pinch of lemon zest. Season well with salt and pepper and wrap up tightly. Repeat for each piece of salmon and place the parcels on a baking tray.

Bake in the oven for 12 to 15 minutes, depending on the size of the fish, so that the salmon is just cooked.

Serve the salmon parcels with couscous, flavoured with a little lemon zest and fresh chopped parsley, and a selection of steamed vegetables.

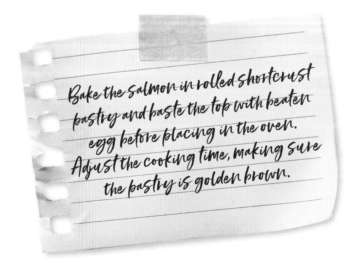

Bake the salmon in rolled shortcrust pastry and baste the top with beaten egg before placing in the oven. Adjust the cooking time, making sure the pastry is golden brown.

Smoked Haddock & Beetroot Quiche

Preparation time: 20-30 minutes | Cooking time: 50 minutes | Serves: 4

I love the haddock in this fresh take on a classic quiche recipe, but you could use hot smoked salmon flakes. The finished quiche can be eaten warm, or enjoyed cold for a summer picnic.

320g ready-rolled shortcrust pastry

2 tablespoons Hawkshead Relish Beetroot & Horseradish Chutney

150g sliced leeks

30g butter

Small bunch of asparagus

180g smoked haddock

100ml cream

5 eggs

Salt and pepper

Chopped chives, to taste

Preheat the oven to 170°c. Line a 24cm quiche dish with the ready-rolled pastry and then blind bake it for 15 to 20 minutes. Remove the baking beans, spread the Beetroot & Horseradish Chutney over the base and then return the quiche to the oven for 5 minutes. Remove and leave to cool slightly while you make the filling.

Soften the leeks in the butter for 4 to 5 minutes then add the asparagus and allow the mixture to cool. Poach the haddock in the cream for 6 minutes and then strain, keeping all the cream, and flake the fish. Whisk the eggs with the cream, salt, pepper and chopped chives.

Layer the leeks and asparagus with the flaked fish in the pastry case, then pour over the cream mixture. Bake the quiche in the preheated oven for 20 to 30 minutes until set. Let it rest for 10 minutes then serve, or leave to cool completely before slicing.

Serve alongside a salad drizzled with a fig & orange dressing on page 122.

If you are not keen on smoked fish, try using crispy bacon instead.

Fig & Orange Jam

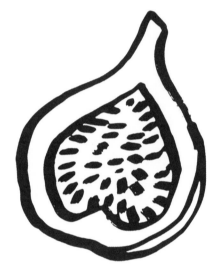

With rich fruity figs and Seville oranges, this is definitely a jam rather than a marmalade. The figs are the main event, perfectly complemented by the oranges and a little lemon zest.

This gorgeous jam is inspired by my parents' travels in southern Spain during our winters, and the many trips Mark and I made to Spain with our girls over the years.

We have fond memories of popping out to the local market on Sunday mornings, dipping churros into thick hot chocolate as we waited for our lunch of spit roast chicken infused with garlic and rosemary to cook. Once it was ready, we'd rush back from the market laden with salads and of course the delicious hot chicken, eager to just tuck in – the scent was heavenly – and we'd simply feast on it under the shade of the surrounding orange trees and wash it all down with the odd glass of wine.

On one of these foraging trips we found a jar of fig jam with orange. It rapidly became a firm favourite, especially when we used it for making a salad dressing to serve alongside the roast chicken.

Our Fig & Orange Jam is so versatile; I love it blended down with a little water to create a glaze to cover a big ham. The little seeds of the fig give it such a great texture, and the flavour really works with both sweet and savoury dishes.

EMBELLISH
WITH RELISH
Fig
and
Orange
jam
great
taste
award
winner
HAWKSHEAD Relish COMPANY

Fruity Fig & Orange Gammon Steaks

Preparation time: 5 minutes | Cooking time: 10 minutes | Serves: 4

This is a very quick and tasty supper dish that's simple to prepare. You can use the Fig & Orange Jam to glaze a whole piece of ham – we often do our Christmas ham with it – and the texture of the crunchy figs with the sweet orange cuts nicely through the saltiness of the gammon.

2 thick gammon steaks

Salt and pepper

2 tablespoons Hawkshead Relish Fig & Orange Jam

2 teaspoons honey

1 teaspoon mustard powder

3 teaspoons Hawkshead Relish Worcester Sauce

To serve

Steamed and crushed new potatoes

Green beans

Season the meat with salt and pepper then preheat a griddle pan until smoking.

Combine the Fig & Orange Jam, honey, mustard powder and Worcester Sauce to make the glaze. Sear the gammon steaks for 4 minutes on each side and then pour over the glaze, coating the steaks. Cook for a further 2 minutes, allowing the glaze to caramelise, then remove from the pan.

Serve with crushed new potatoes and green beans.

If you think the gammon may be too salty, soak it for at least an hour in water before cooking, or overnight if you can, rinsing it prior to cooking.

Always good with a fried egg on top!

Summer Ham Hock & Asparagus Salad

Preparation time: 20 minutes | Cooking time: 5 minutes | Serves: 4

A fabulous celebration of summer on a plate. I love fresh, thin, new season asparagus. With the soft-boiled eggs, shredded ham, orange segments and thinly shaved fennel this salad packs a punch on the taste buds and works a treat with the sticky fruity dressing.

200g cooked ham hock

Bunch of asparagus

4 free-range eggs

6 thinly sliced radishes

1 thinly sliced red onion

1 thinly sliced small bulb of fennel

1 segmented or sliced orange

Salad leaves of your choice

For the dressing

2 tablespoons Hawkshead Relish Fig & Orange Jam

1 tablespoon olive oil

1 tablespoon white wine vinegar

Salt and pepper

½ teaspoon Hawkshead Relish Dijon mustard

Shred the cooked ham hock into large chunks; this works best if the ham is still slightly warm rather than hot. If taking from the fridge, let it come up to room temperature before serving.

Cook the asparagus in salted boiling water until just al dente then allow to cool slightly.

Boil the eggs for 7 to 8 minutes then immediately pop them under cold running water, or into a bowl of iced water, to stop them cooking further. After a couple of minutes, peel away the shell and cut into quarters.

Build the salad on a large serving platter using all the ingredients.

For the dressing

Put all the ingredients in a jar and shake well to combine. Drizzle over the salad and serve.

Would work beautifully with prawns, crispy bacon or pancetta if you don't have ham to hand.

Fig & Orange Glazed Duck

Preparation time: 30 minutes | Cooking time: 90 minutes | Serves: 4

Orange with duck is a match made in heaven, and this dish devised by Martin Frickel really brings out the flavours of the fruit and spices. Matched with his fabulous braised red cabbage it's a real treat, and the perfect showstopper for family and friends at any time of the year.

2.8kg Goosnargh duck

Salt and pepper

1 tablespoon vegetable oil

For the red cabbage

1 small red cabbage

Zest of 1 orange

300ml red wine

1 teaspoon Hawkshead Relish Worcester Sauce

70ml red wine vinegar

2 tablespoons Hawkshead Relish Redcurrant Jelly

For the glaze

150g honey

150g Hawkshead Relish Fig & Orange Jam

45ml red wine vinegar

5g salt

1 beef stock pot

1 teaspoon mustard seeds

1 teaspoon fennel seeds

10g thyme leaves

Preheat the oven to 210°c.

For the red cabbage

Finely slice the red cabbage and place into a large saucepan with the orange zest, red wine, Worcester Sauce and red wine vinegar. Cover with a lid and simmer for 30 minutes, stirring occasionally, and then add the Redcurrant Jelly and cook for a further 10 minutes until soft and sticky.

For the glaze

Combine all the ingredients in a small saucepan and simmer for 10 minutes until reduced and sticky, then leave to cool slightly.

Season the whole duck with salt and pepper, making sure the skin is nice and dry. Brush the oil over the skin then place the duck into the preheated oven for 7 minutes breast side up. Turn over and roast for another 7 minutes, then remove from the oven and heavily brush the glaze all over the duck. Return to the oven for 20 minutes breast side up, brushing with the glaze every 5 minutes.

Leave the duck to rest in a warm place for 25 minutes before serving it with the braised red cabbage, potatoes roasted in duck fat, roast carrots and wilted greens.

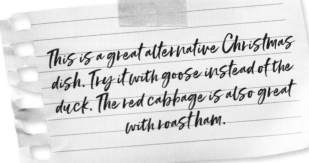

This is a great alternative Christmas dish. Try it with goose instead of the duck. The red cabbage is also great with roast ham.

Fruity Fig Baklava

Preparation time: 15-20 minutes | Cooking time: 1 hour | Serves: 4

Baklava can be a fiddle to make if you are making your own pastry, but frankly life is too short and the ready-made versions are great. This version was inspired by Chris, our technical manager, who loves his baklava and is quite the aficionado.

500g pistachios

3 tablespoons sugar

175g unsalted butter

100ml sunflower oil

2 tablespoons Hawkshead Relish Fig & Orange Jam

500g filo pastry

For the syrup

100g sugar

250ml water

Juice of ½ a lemon

2 teaspoons Hawkshead Relish Fig & Orange Jam

Preheat the oven to 180°c.

Grind or chop the nuts and blend with the sugar. Melt the butter, combine it with the oil and pour four tablespoons of the mixture over the chopped nuts. Add the Fig & Orange Jam and mix well.

Grease a 30cm baking tin or ovenproof dish with some of the remaining oil and butter mixture. Lay half of the pastry sheets into the dish one at a time, brushing each layer with the oil and butter mixture. Make sure you ease the pastry into all the corners.

Spread the nut mix across the top in an even layer and cover with the remaining pastry, making sure you brush each layer with the rest of the melted butter and oil mix.

Once all the layers have been completed, score lines in the pastry to create diamond shapes of about 5 to 6cm each.

Bake in the oven for around 1 hour until the top is crisp and golden.

For the syrup

Simmer the sugar, water, lemon juice and jam for around 10 minutes and then leave to cool.

When the baklava is ready, pour the cooled syrup along the score lines in the pastry so it seeps through, then return it to the oven for a further 5 minutes.

Remove from the oven and allow to cool fully before slicing along the score lines and serving.

Fig & Orange Brioche Pudding

Preparation time: 10-15 minutes | Cooking time: 45 minutes | Serves: 4

Using brioche or leftover panettone elevates this bread and butter pudding to a whole new level for the 21st century. You just need a great custard to serve with it! Eat either hot or cold; it will keep for a few days, if it lasts long enough that is!

6 slices of brioche (can use leftover panettone or good quality white bread without the crusts)

50g softened butter

4 or 5 tablespoons Hawkshead Relish Fig & Orange Jam

275ml whole milk

60ml double cream

3 large eggs

75g sugar

Zest of 1 orange

25g candied peel

75g sultanas

1 teaspoon Demerara sugar

To serve

Custard

Whipped cream, with a little orange liqueur folded through

Preheat the oven to 170°c.

Generously butter the slices of brioche, panettone or bread on one side and then spread three tablespoons of jam over them. Cut the slices into triangles and arrange them in an ovenproof baking dish butter side up, overlapping as you go and keeping them stood up if you can.

Whisk together the milk, cream, eggs, sugar and half the orange zest then pour this mixture over the bread. Scatter the candied peel, sultanas, Demerara sugar and remaining orange zest over the pudding, then leave it to soak for 20 minutes.

Place in the preheated oven for 40 to 45 minutes until the top is golden and crunchy, then brush more jam over the top and cook for a further 5 minutes.

Serve the pudding straight from the oven with custard or whipped cream with a little orange liqueur folded through.

Use brandy, rum or an orange liqueur such as Grand Marnier or Cointreau folded through the cream or added to the mix along with the jam.

Raspberry & Vanilla Jam

A classic Victoria sponge, made with vanilla extract and a great raspberry jam filling, was the inspiration for this preserve. We all know that this classic combination works so well together... a perfect match, you might say. The vanilla brings out the intensity of the raspberries, reminiscent of a great raspberry ripple ice cream.

This was the first jam that we created, to serve with the scones we made in our Hawkshead café. For me, this flavour combination is the taste of a perfect afternoon tea, which is why we've included recipes for a classic Victoria sponge and simply delicious scones in this chapter.

If you fancy being a little daring, you could add a teaspoon of Raspberry and Vanilla Jam to a glass of prosecco or even a gin and tonic... simply add and give it a stir to bring a lovely sweet flavour to the tipple of your choice.

You will also find it works especially well in a rich dark chocolate cake with a layer of the jam running right through the middle, topped off with handful of fresh whole raspberries added for texture.

EMBELLISH
WITH RELISH

Raspberry
and
Vanilla
jam

great
taste

HAWKSHEAD *Relish* COMPANY

Afternoon Tea

Preparation time: 30 minutes | Cooking time: 45 minutes | Serves: 8-10

An afternoon tea, with freshly baked warm fruit scones and a traditional Victoria sponge with Raspberry & Vanilla Jam, is a delight that everyone can appreciate. I would always go butter, then jam, then cream on my scone (pronounced to rhyme with gone, as they very quickly are!)

For the Victoria sponge

4 eggs

225g caster sugar

225g self-raising flour

2 teaspoons baking powder

225g softened butter

½ vanilla pod

110g Hawkshead Relish Raspberry & Vanilla Jam

Icing sugar, for dusting

For the scones

500g plain flour

2 large eggs beaten

100g caster sugar

125g softened butter

65g mixed dried fruit

250ml milk

25g baking powder

For the Victoria sponge

Preheat the oven to 180°c.

Break the eggs into a bowl and add the sugar, flour, baking powder and butter. Scrape out the vanilla seeds and add them to the bowl, then mix well using a hand-held mixer.

Divide the batter equally between two greased and lined 20cm sandwich cake tins. Bake in the centre of the oven for 25 minutes or until golden and springy to the touch.

Leave the sponges to cool in the tins for 5 minutes then carefully move to a wire rack. Once cooled completely, turn one cake over and spread the underside with a thick layer of the Raspberry & Vanilla Jam. Top with the second cake and dust with icing sugar.

For the scones

Preheat the oven to 190°c.

Sift the flour and baking powder into a bowl, stir in the sugar then rub in the butter to breadcrumb consistency. Sprinkle in the dried fruit and pour in the beaten egg with three tablespoons of the milk. Bring together using a round-bladed knife to form a soft sticky dough, then place on a lightly floured worktop. Roll into a long tube like a swiss roll then cut into approximately 3 to 4cm rounds.

Place the scones on a greased baking tray. Brush with a little milk, dust with a sprinkle of flour and place on the top shelf of the oven for 12 to 15 minutes until they are golden brown.

Remove a tub of ice cream from the freezer and allow to soften very slightly, then stir in a tablespoon of Raspberry & Vanilla Jam. Return it to the freezer, elevating a plain vanilla to a succulent Raspberry Ripple.

Queen of Puddings

Preparation time: 30 minutes | Cooking time: 40 minutes | Serves: 4

Anyone who did domestic science at school and is of a certain age, shall we say, will probably remember making this. The height of sophistication back then, I might add! With the layer of Raspberry & Vanilla Jam, this is actually a great resurrection from the past.

For the base

200g ready-made swiss roll

3 eggs

80g caster sugar

250ml milk

250ml cream

1 vanilla pod

1 jar of Hawkshead Relish Raspberry & Vanilla Jam

For the topping

3 egg whites

175g caster sugar

Preheat the oven to 160°c while you slice the swiss roll and layer it across the bottom of an ovenproof pudding dish.

Whisk the eggs and sugar in a bowl until creamy. Place the milk and cream in a saucepan, split the vanilla pod and scrape out the seeds into the pan, add the pod itself and bring the liquid to the point of boiling. Remove the vanilla pod then whisk the hot liquid into the eggs and sugar until well combined.

Pour the custard over the swiss roll and allow it to soak into the cake for around 20 minutes.

Half fill a larger roasting tin with hot water and place the pudding dish in the tray; the water level should reach halfway up the sides of the dish.

Bake for 20 to 25 minutes then remove from the oven once the custard is set. Allow it to cool slightly then spoon over a generous layer of the Raspberry & Vanilla Jam.

To make the meringue, whisk the egg whites to stiff peaks and then slowly add the sugar, a spoonful at a time, while whisking until you have a thick glossy consistency. If you have a piping bag you can pipe the meringue over the top, if not use a spoon to pull it upwards into peaks.

Place the dish under a hot grill for 4 to 6 minutes until the meringue is lovely and browned. You can use a blowtorch instead if you have one.

Can be made in individual ramekins for a retro dinner party dessert.

Raspberry & White Chocolate Slice

Preparation time: 15 minutes | Cooking time: 45 minutes | Serves: 8-10

Almost too good... if you can resist eating them all yourself these are a great crowd pleaser. The combination of a pastry base, crumble topping and white chocolate drizzle is divine!

115g melted unsalted butter

50g granulated sugar

¼ teaspoon salt

125g plain flour

200g Hawkshead Relish Raspberry & Vanilla Jam

10-12 fresh raspberries

40g large oats

70g light brown sugar

½ teaspoon cinnamon

30g plain flour

60g chilled and diced unsalted butter

50g white chocolate

Preheat the oven to 150°c and line a shallow baking tin with baking parchment.

Stir the melted butter, granulated sugar and salt together in a bowl, then add the plain flour and stir until just combined. Press into the prepared tray and bake for 15 minutes.

Spread the jam over the base in a thick layer and dot with fresh raspberries, reserving some for the top. Whisk the oats, brown sugar, cinnamon and plain flour together in a bowl. Add the chilled butter and mix with your fingers to a breadcrumb texture. Scatter this crumble mixture over the jam layer, then sprinkle over the remaining raspberries.

Bake for 30 minutes until the topping turns golden brown and the jam is bubbling through.

Leave to cool for around 20 minutes then chill in the fridge for a couple of hours to set. Melt the white chocolate and drizzle lightly over the bake. Chill for another few minutes to set, then cut into squares or bars as you prefer.

Store in an airtight box for up to a week (they really won't last that long!).

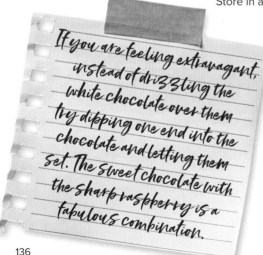

If you are feeling extravagant, instead of drizzling the white chocolate over them try dipping one end into the chocolate and letting them set. The sweet chocolate with the sharp raspberry is a fabulous combination.

Raspberry Bakewell Tart

Preparation time: 20 minutes | Cooking time: 35-40 minutes | Serves: 8-10

My dad had a real sweet tooth and loved his Bakewell tarts. This recipe is a variation that gives you the look and feel of a traditional Bakewell, but with a layer of jam and whole raspberries dotted throughout the mix, it's divine.

For the pastry

200g plain flour

2 tablespoons icing sugar

100g cold cubed butter

1 medium egg

1 teaspoon lemon juice

Splash of cold water

For the filling

100g unsalted butter

100g caster sugar

2 large eggs

50g plain flour

75g ground almonds

100g Hawkshead Relish Raspberry & Vanilla Jam

100g fresh raspberries

20g flaked almonds

Dusting of icing sugar

Heat the oven to 200°c.

For the pastry

Mix the flour and icing sugar with the butter to get a breadcrumb-like texture. Combine the egg, lemon juice and a little cold water then add this to the mix, with a touch more water if needed to bring the pastry together. Form it into a ball, wrap in cling film and chill in the fridge for 20 minutes.

Grease a 23cm round or rectangular baking dish, then roll out the chilled pastry to about half a centimetre thickness and line the dish. Leave any excess hanging over the edge as it will shrink in the oven. Prick the pastry base with a fork, cover with baking parchment and fill with baking beans.

Place in the preheated oven and blind bake for 12 to 15 minutes, then remove the beans and paper and return the pastry case to the oven for a further 5 minutes to dry out. Trim off the overhanging edges then allow to cool.

For the filling

Beat the butter and sugar together until light and fluffy, slowly beat in the eggs and then stir in the flour and almonds.

Spread the base of the tart with a good layer of Raspberry & Vanilla Jam, scatter over a few of the fresh raspberries, pour over the frangipane filling and shake gently to evenly spread out.

Bake in the oven for 10 minutes then scatter the flaked almonds on the top and cook for a further 15 minutes until golden brown.

Leave to cool slightly, dust with icing sugar, and then transfer to a wire rack to completely cool.

Make individual ones for a tea party. For a change, drizzle a little dark chocolate over the top once cooked and allow to set.

Raspberry Cranachan

Preparation time: 5 minutes | Cooking time: 15 minutes | Serves: 4

This takes me back to the days when Mark and I ran the Queen's Head in Hawkshead and this dessert was often on the menu. It was always very popular, although we didn't have Raspberry & Vanilla Jam in those days, and deliciously rich and decadent with the added whisky finish.

30g caster sugar

100g coarse oatmeal

300g fresh raspberries

1½ tablespoons Hawkshead Relish Raspberry & Vanilla Jam

3 tablespoons whisky

300ml whipping cream

Mint leaves, for decoration

Place the caster sugar in a pan with one and a half tablespoons of water. Leave on a low heat for around 5 minutes to melt. Do not stir.

Put the oatmeal in a frying pan on a medium heat and swirl it around to brown, but don't let it burn. Once it has started to colour, remove from the heat.

Once the sugar has dissolved, increase the heat and bring to a boil until it turns the colour of honey, then stir in the oatmeal and spread the mixture on an oiled baking sheet to cool.

Once it has cooled and set, break into pieces, or pop in a small food processor for a quick whizz.

Place the raspberries in a saucepan (keeping a few back for decoration) with the Raspberry & Vanilla Jam and heat until they start to break down.

Add the whisky to the cream and whip until thick and holding its shape. Reserve a couple of tablespoons of the oatmeal mix, and stir the rest through the cream.

Put a heaped tablespoon of the cream in a glass or dish, followed by the same of raspberry jam, then add more cream and another raspberry layer. Sprinkle over a little of the oatmeal mix, and top with a fresh raspberry and a mint leaf. Chill until ready to serve.

Makes a great filling for meringues. Use yoghurt instead of cream for a lighter mix.

Salted Caramel Sauce

In Brittany, northern France, they have long made caramel using their salted butter, and by the late 1990s that had evolved into this wonderful, heady sauce.

Our version is simply an adaptation of a sticky toffee sauce that we had already created and still make to this day. However, including the finest sea salt available anywhere in the world – created by Halen Môn in Anglesey – elevates our sauce way above any other. Using this ultra-pure sea salt means that the balance between sweet and salty flavours in our sauce is just perfect.

One very well-known food writer and critic came to visit us on a day we were making this, and he set off on the train back to London with a jar still warm from the pan. Later he messaged me to show me an empty jar; he'd polished off the lot on the way home!

Apart from drizzling our Salted Caramel Sauce over ice cream or sticky toffee pudding, you can spoon it through custard, serve it with pancakes or waffles, and stir it into a latte or even a hot chocolate. One of our simple favourites is to fry a peeled and sliced banana in a little butter, and when the butter starts to sizzle and the banana is hot, spoon over a little of the sauce then serve straight away with ice cream.

You could even try a cheeky Salted Caramel Espresso Martini: stir two teaspoons of the sauce into 50ml of vodka, pour in an espresso and simply add ice and shake, then serve in a Martini glass.

Or you can just eat it straight from the jar!

EMBELLISH
WITH RELISH
Salted Caramel sauce
Anglesey
HAWKSHEAD Relish COMPANY

Banana & Salted Caramel Showstopper Cake

Preparation time: approx. 35 minutes, plus 1 hour cooling | Baking time: 35 minutes | Serves: 8

We were looking for a 'showstopper' cake to celebrate Hawkshead Relish's 20th anniversary and a visit from HRH The Prince of Wales in April 2019, so I asked Martin Frickel to come up with something spectacular and he did us proud! The sponge is layered with buttercream, then the whole thing is drizzled with salted caramel and topped with caramelised banana. The result was so many great compliments and an empty platter: the proof was most definitely in the eating.

For the cake

300g softened unsalted butter, plus extra for the tins

300g soft light brown sugar

4 large eggs

300g sifted plain flour

2 tablespoons baking powder

1 tablespoon bicarbonate of soda

2 teaspoons vanilla extract

4 ripe mashed bananas

For the caramel buttercream

150g softened unsalted butter

500g icing sugar

200g soft cheese

80g Hawkhead Relish Salted Caramel Sauce

To assemble

150g Hawkhead Relish Salted Caramel Sauce

1 tablespoon cold water

2 ripe bananas

25g unsalted butter

Generous pinch of Halen Môn sea salt flakes

Handful of walnut halves

Preheat the oven to 180°c. Meanwhile, grease and line two deep 20cm springform cake tins using the extra butter and baking paper.

For the cake

Beat the butter and sugar in a large bowl until light and fluffy. Crack in the eggs, one by one, and mix between each addition until thoroughly combined. Fold in the flour, followed by the baking powder and bicarbonate of soda. Stir in the vanilla extract and the mashed bananas until just combined. Divide the batter equally between the lined cake tins and bake in the preheated oven for 35 minutes or until a skewer inserted into the middles comes out clean. Cool in the tins for at least 10 minutes, then transfer to a wire rack to cool completely.

For the caramel buttercream

Beat the butter and icing sugar for 5 minutes or until light and fluffy. Add the soft cheese and beat for another minute or until fully combined. Add the Salted Caramel Sauce and mix until the buttercream is thick yet spreadable.

To assemble

Spread 50g of the Salted Caramel Sauce on top of one of the sponges, followed by a thick layer of the buttercream, then chill for 10 minutes. Put the plain sponge on top of the iced one and spread the remaining buttercream over the top and sides of the cake. Chill for at least 30 minutes.

In a bowl, whisk the remaining 100g of caramel with the cold water until smooth. Slice the bananas at an angle while you melt the butter in a frying pan. Fry the sliced bananas for 2 to 3 minutes or until they begin to caramelise. Cool and then gently stir through half of the whisked caramel.

Put the cake on a serving plate or stand and pile the caramelised bananas on top, then drizzle with the remaining caramel. Sprinkle with a few sea salt flakes and add some walnut halves if you like.

Sticky Toffee Pudding

Preparation time: 10 minutes | Cooking time: 40 minutes | Serves: 4

Mark proposed to me over this pudding at the Miller Howe Hotel in Bowness. Chef patron John Tovey gave me a copy of his recipe, which I still think is the best version, so it's often copied and rarely bettered, except of course with lashings of our Salted Caramel Sauce and extra sea salt flakes on top which look like little jewels.

60g softened butter

85g soft brown sugar

2 lightly beaten eggs

120g self-raising flour

1 teaspoon bicarbonate of soda

1 freshly made espresso

120g stoned and chopped dates

To serve

1 jar of Hawkshead Relish Salted Caramel Sauce

Halen Môn sea salt flakes

Vanilla ice cream

Heat the oven to 180°c and line an 18cm loose-bottomed cake tin with greaseproof paper.

Cream together the butter and sugar then gradually add the eggs until combined. Fold in the flour and bicarbonate of soda.

Pour the coffee over the dates, stir together then add to the cake mixture. It should be quite runny; if not add a little warm water.

Pour into the tin, place that on a baking sheet and bake for 30 to 40 minutes until springy to the touch.

To serve

Warm the contents of a jar of Salted Caramel Sauce. To do this, either remove the lid and pop in a microwave for 20 seconds, stir, then heat for another 20 seconds until warm and runny, or empty the contents into a pan and place on a low heat to gently warm through, but do not allow to boil.

Sprinkle each slice of sticky toffee pudding with a few large flakes of Halen Môn sea salt, add a scoop of good vanilla ice cream and drizzle with the warm Salted Caramel Sauce.

To enhance the ice cream, remove it from the freezer and allow it to defrost very slightly, then add a spoonful of Salted Caramel Sauce, swirl round and pop back in the freezer for later.

Salted Caramel Apple Parcels

Preparation time: 40 minutes | Cooking time: 35 minutes | Serves: 4

Sunday dinner would always mean a pudding, which was usually served with homemade custard. One of my favourites was simply baked apples; my job was to use the apple corer to remove the centre and then pack it with mixed fruits and pop it in the oven. I've worked with Martin Frickel to recreate this taste of my youth as an elegant and delicious dessert.

170g dried mixed fruit

Zest of 1 orange

1 tablespoon gingerbread rum (or alcohol of your choice)

1 jar of Hawkshead Relish Salted Caramel Sauce

4 Braeburn apples

200g shortcrust pastry

25g butter

2 beaten eggs

Combine the dried fruit, orange zest, alcohol and four tablespoons of Salted Caramel Sauce. Leave that to soak for 30 minutes.

Peel and core the apples then stuff the centres with the soaked fruit mix and brush the apples with Salted Caramel Sauce.

Preheat the oven to 180°c.

Cut the pastry into four 10cm squares and top each with one tablespoon of Salted Caramel Sauce and a stuffed apple. Top with a small cube of butter and a blob of Salted Caramel Sauce, then fold the four corners of the pastry inwards to cover the apple. Rest the parcels in the fridge for 10 to 15 minutes then brush with beaten egg.

Bake in the preheated oven for 25 to 30 minutes until browned. Serve with custard and an extra drizzle of Salted Caramel Sauce.

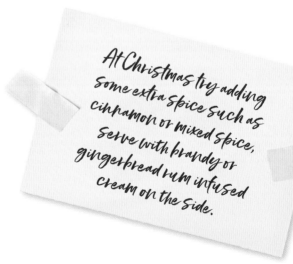

At Christmas try adding some extra spice such as cinnamon or mixed spice, serve with brandy or gingerbread rum infused cream on the side.

Salted Caramel Brownie

Preparation time: 10 minutes | Cooking time: 30 minutes | Serves: 8-10

Everyone loves a brownie, don't they? This one with salted caramel is sweet, moist and sticky. You can serve it as a cake with your morning coffee or with a light custard as a pudding; either way it's rich, delicious and very moreish.

250g unsalted butter

200g dark chocolate (50-70% cocoa)

4 eggs

370g caster sugar

80g cocoa powder

60g plain flour

½ teaspoon baking powder

100g walnut halves (optional)

1 jar of Hawkshead Relish Salted Caramel Sauce

Halen Môn sea salt flakes

Heat the oven to 160°c. Grease and line a 23cm square tin with baking parchment.

Melt the butter in a pan and break in the chocolate, then remove from the heat and allow the chocolate to slowly melt. Allow to cool gently.

Whisk the eggs and sugar until they have doubled in size using a hand-held mixer. Add the cooled chocolate mix then fold in the dry ingredients, including the walnuts if using but reserve a few for the top.

Pour half the batter into the tin, pour over a layer of the Salted Caramel Sauce, then finish with another layer of the chocolate brownie mix. Scatter a few walnut halves and Halen Môn salt crystals over the top and bake for 20 to 25 minutes until risen and the top is glossy and cracked.

Let the brownie cool completely in the tin before cutting into squares.

Add a splash of your favourite tipple to the mix for added indulgence, rum, brandy or whisky all work well.

Salted Caramel Popcorn Slice

Preparation time: 10 minutes | Cooking time: 10 minutes | Serves: 4

Popcorn is a great favourite of ours, especially with Salted Caramel Sauce. This is a quick no-bake treat that is perfect for the kids' lunch boxes and one they will love to help you make. It's just a simple task of combining everything and leaving the mixture to set, then washing up... after licking the bowl, of course!

50g butter

75g Hawkshead Relish Salted Caramel Sauce

200g marshmallows

80g salted popcorn

50g Rice Krispies

50g peanuts

50g melted dark chocolate

Halen Môn sea salt

Lightly grease and line a 25cm baking tray.

Place the butter and Salted Caramel Sauce in a saucepan and gently warm as you stir them together. Add the marshmallows and let them melt a little, then add the popcorn, Rice Krispies and peanuts. Mix until everything is coated.

Transfer to the tray, pressing the mixture down and into the corners evenly. Leave to cool and set in the fridge, then cut into squares and drizzle the melted dark chocolate over the top. Dress with a few Halen Môn sea salt crystals or flakes to finish.

Royal Visits

In 2011, myself and Mark were both awarded MBEs for services to the food industry in Cumbria. They were on HRH The Queen's Birthday Honours list, and we received them at Buckingham Palace in the November of that year. The MBEs were in recognition of our company having worked closely with other food producers in Cumbria, and promoting the regional food offer. We had also advised the government in the capacity of running a small business, and assisted them in completing the UK Food & Drink Export Plan together with DEFRA and UKTI (UK Trade and Investment) with the aim of helping other small businesses to export.

2019 marked the 20th year of Hawkshead Relish, and welcoming HRH The Prince of Wales to our production facility at Esthwaite was a highlight that we will never forget. Not only did he meet us and all the Relish family, but he took the time to chat to everyone and even had a go at jarring some chutney in the kitchen. Judging by his smiles on the day, he enjoyed it as much as we did!

Halen Môn

How We Met

Back in 2006, my mum and dad took the girls to Anglesey with their caravan. We couldn't get away easily in the summer holidays as the business was growing and just too busy, however we did manage a couple of days where we nipped down and joined them. On one such occasion we took them to visit the Sea Zoo, based on the Menai Straits, and as we left a lady dashed across the car park wanting to know if we were 'The Hawkshead Relish' which made us laugh, as we had no idea anyone knew of us. We had a wheel cover on the back of the car with our logo, which she had seen and wanted to know if she could stock our products in her shop after seeing us at the Great Taste Awards. That lady turned out to be Alison Lea Wilson, who with her husband David went on to found Halen Môn, the sea salt company based in Anglesey. We've become good friends since then, and now make a few products exclusively for them, as well as using Halen Môn in many of our Hawkshead Relish products. It's so beautiful and pure, I wouldn't have it any other way, and I would never use anything else at home either.

The Halen Môn Story

In 1997, we left a saucepan of seawater to boil on the Aga in our family kitchen and as the salt crystals started to form, we knew we'd struck culinary gold. In 1999, we started supplying Halen Môn Sea Salt to Swains, our local butchers in Menai Bridge on the Isle of Anglesey.

Today, our sea salt is enjoyed around the world by chefs, food lovers and even Barack Obama. It has been served at the London 2012 Olympics, political summits and royal weddings and is a vital ingredient in lots of well-known brands, including our very favourite relishers, Hawkshead.

We love working with companies like Mark and Maria's – people who care deeply about what they make and how they make it. You can find our salt on their shop shelves, as well as in hundreds of the nation's best delicatessens. Find out more at www.halenmon.com.

Kendal College & Martin Frickel

Hawkshead Relish have been working with the Kendal College Culinary team and their students for about ten years now. We've sponsored events, provided work experience opportunities and worked with their students to develop their knowledge and skills.

We really admire what the college team have done to raise the status of catering as a career through their solid reputation and consistent high standards of sheer hard work. Every establishment in the area knows they're getting someone of quality and ability when they take on a Kendal College Culinary student.

The college team are passionate about food and the provenance of the ingredients they use, keeping up to date with food trends and covering all aspects from foraging to fine dining. There is no doubt at all that the Kendal College Culinary team, led by Richard Axford, are creating the chefs of the future.

They are very proactive when it comes to supporting and developing these talented students. Even when finances present obstacles the team come up with innovative ways to ensure their students can study and learn as much as possible.

Thanks to their bursary and fundraising schemes, which we continue to support, the college has been able to take students to a range of countries around the world to discover other cuisines and cultures, to broaden their knowledge and experience of food. Those chefs who've been fortunate to participate in these trips have all said that it was the absolute making of them.

Inevitably, not all culinary students want to go on and work in either a hotel or restaurant environment; some want to work in food product development. We've been lucky enough to be able to help a number of students in this area by providing them with opportunities to experience and work in a food production facility and a development kitchen. Many of the college's current students have been involved in testing and developing the recipes in this book and creating those dishes for the photos: a great learning experience for all involved.

Alongside this, we've also had the pleasure of working with Kendal College Culinary Alumnus, Martin Frickel. A former pupil of Kirkbie Kendal School, he later trained as a chef at the college and, since graduating, has worked in some of Cumbria's most illustrious kitchens including L'enclume in Cartmel and Forest Side in Grasmere.

We were thrilled when Martin agreed to help us with this book; he has been invaluable in testing every recipe and even contributing a few of his own creations made with our range of products. Between us, we hope that we have created a cookbook that will inspire you to get creative in your own kitchens.

Richard Axford, Martin Frickel and the Kendal culinary team students

Martin Frickel with Craig Noble

Catherine Conner working
her magic on the styling

Embellish WITH RELISH

©2019 Meze Publishing Ltd.
All rights reserved.
First edition printed in 2019 in the UK
ISBN: 978-1-910863-49-7
Written by: Maria Whitehead MBE
Photography by: Tim Green
(www.timgreenphotographer.com)
Edited by: Katie Fisher, Phil Turner
Proof reading: Chris Brierley
Designed by: Paul Cocker, Izzy Whitehead
Contributors: Ruth Alexander, George Carrick,
Michael Johnson, Sarah Koriba, Marek
Nowicki, Victoria Sedgwick, Anna Tebble,
Emma Toogood, Sophie Westgate

Hawkshead Relish Company
Esthwaite Old Hall Barns
Esthwaite
Hawkshead
Cumbria LA22 0QF
Web: www.hawksheadrelish.com
Telephone: 015394 36614
Email: info@hawksheadrelish.com

Meze Publishing Limited
Unit 1b, 2 Kelham Square
Kelham Riverside
Sheffield S3 8SD
Web: www.mezepublishing.co.uk
Telephone: 0114 275 7709
Email: info@mezepublishing.co.uk

HAWKSHEAD *Relish* COMPANY

me:ze PUBLISHING